KEITH KENNEDY

Rules To The Game

THE Hip-Hop Entrepreneur's Guide To Hustling

MANIFEST DESTINY

PUBLICATIONS

First edition

ISBN: 978-1-7358016-0-5

Editing by Stephen Kennedy
Best Brother: Marcus Kennedy

This book is dedicated w/luv to those who are striving to be the best version of themselves. You can do it!

Special thanks to those that love me the most - Marcus, Kamilah, Dad, Margo, Jaia, Austyn, JB and Mahogani* for the inspiration, motivation & encouragement. I could not have done this without you. You are the bestest!

Thanks to all those that helped me in my journey & you for buying or just reading this book. Pass it on.

Hi Mom, I did it! I finally got a book published like you! :)

Contents

1

TL; DR – TOO LONG; DIDN'T READ

This is a summary of the chapters within **RULES TO THE GAME** in case you need a quick reference guide.

CHAPTER 1 - *TL; DR - TOO LONG; DIDN'T READ*

CHAPTER 2 – *ALLOW ME TO RE-INTRODUCE MYSELF*

The Game can only be played by you, your way. There will be many challenges, but if you persevere and stay consistent, you can win.

CHAPTER 3 – *WITH A LITTLE HELP FROM MY FRIENDS*

You will not be able to win if you do it by yourself. Having a strong support system of friends, family and colleagues will go a long way to your success. A few of mine have blessed us with their knowledge and experiences for you to learn from.

CHAPTER 4 – *DON'T BE SCURRED – LEAP OF FAITH*

It's never too late to change. But, first you must decide to take that leap of faith and keep moving forward on whatever path that you have determined it to be.

CHAPTER 5 – *PLAN ACCORDINGLY*

In order for you to be successful, you must first come up with a project then plan it out accordingly. Find the time to get it done regardless of the obstacles.

CHAPTER 6 – *STOP PROCRASTINATING — GET' ER DONE!!!*

Understand that time waits for no one. It is the most precious resource because it is finite. Once it is gone, there is no getting it back, ever. You must decide how you want to spend your time and who you want to spend it with. Father time is undefeated. You must make time for what you want, don't waste it. Do what needs to be done and greatness will soon follow. Langston Hughes said, "a dream deferred is a dream denied." Stop denying yourself the ability to live your dreams. Now is the time to get 'er done!

CHAPTER 7 – *PUT SOME RESPECT ON MY NAME*

Respect is a two way street that must never be violated. If so, expect strong repercussions. Or as OG Magnum summarizes, "respect everyone, even the one's cleaning up the rooms after you. You have to see all of the people around you and never consider anyone less or greater than yourself."

CHAPTER 8 – *COMMUNICATION IS KEY*

Proper communication can be difficult, but it is necessary to master these tools to win The Game. People will remember the feelings of how you said something more than what was actually said. As such, always leave on a positive note.

CHAPTER 9 – *I GOT THE HOOK UP – RELATIONSHIPS*

Relationships are the lifeblood to The Game. Create, cultivate, nurture and protect them because your life depends on it.

CHAPTER 10 – *WHAT TIME IS IT!?...GAME TIME!!*

To play The Game, sometimes you have to play the game. Have fun and remember good sportsmanship, win or lose, because a potential relationship is on the line.

CHAPTER 11 – *I HAVE THE POWER*

Power can be attained through careful planning and execution, but it is precarious. Just when you think you have it, it can slip from your grasp. Always protect what you have as you reach for more. Power is a 0 sum game. If you are gaining it, someone is losing it. Be aware that the powerful will always fight to retain what they have. Power is a tool to be used as necessary, for good or for evil, is up to you.

CHAPTER 12 – *TAKE ME TO YOUR LEADER*

Being a leader can be difficult, thankless and lonely. Since you can't win alone, you must be able to extend your reach and expand in The Game through strong leadership. When all else fails, act with purpose and speak with conviction (even if you have no idea what to do next). Most people will follow you until you give them a reason not to.

CHAPTER 13 – *TAKING AN L*

Life is often cruel with the lessons it teaches after the test. Understand if you play The Game long enough, eventually it will be your turn to take an L. Know that the harder the L, the better the lesson taught and the stronger your bounce back will be.

CHAPTER 14 – *WHAT'S MY MOTIVATION?*

Start your day by looking at yourself in the mirror and proclaiming out loud how great you are. How great this day will be. How no one can "f" with you, because you are the baddest one walking in the jungle. Whatever you need to tell yourself to fire you up, do it. There are too many things in the world ready to tear you down, the world doesn't need you to do it for them. Claim the day before it starts to get it going the right way!

CHAPTER 15 – *LET'S MAKE A DEAL*

If you are to sign your life away, make sure it is on your terms.

CHAPTER 16 – *SHOW ME THE MONEY*

Money and a fool are soon parted. Embrace these tips to make sure you have a strong foundation to build wealth that lasts, not just money to blow.

CHAPTER 17 – *MIND, BODY & SPIRIT*

You will not go far in The Game without a sound mind, body and spirit. Take the steps necessary to keep them healthy so you can win.

CHAPTER 18 – *RANDOM RULES*

These are just some thoughts and nuggets of knowledge that need to be shared but didn't fit into the flow of the book.

2

ALLOW ME TO RE-INTRODUCE MYSELF

"I've been in this game for years, it's made me an animal
It's rules to this sh!t, I wrote me a manual
A step by step booklet / For you to get your game on track
Not your wig pushed back"

NOTORIOUS B.I.G. - *"10 Crack Commandments"*

* * *

Greetings Fellow Hustler!

Thank you for taking time to pick up my book, **_RULES TO THE GAME_**. To paraphrase the great American poet, Jay-Z, you could be reading about anything in the world, but you're reading with me. I appreciate that! :)

RULES TO THE GAME is a collection of my thoughts, lessons, and perspectives gleaned from nearly 25 years of music / entertainment experience and

40+ years of life. I have also included notes on worldly examples to help support key points. Plus, I have been blessed enough to gain access to various industry tastemakers to help share their wisdom as well. Even though you can lead a horse to water, you can't make it drink. As such, it's up to you to use this knowledge accordingly. In fact, I encourage you to use the margins and notes section of this book to write down random thoughts, anything you learned, or the next steps you plan to take for your desires. The more ink, the better!

Forgive me, where are my manners? Who am I? My name is Keith Kennedy. My story is one of high hopes, dreams, successes, failures and everything in between driven from the sole motivation to be my own boss. Perhaps like you, I never wanted nor was I ever good at slaving away in a cubicle or being micromanaged by others with small minds and even worse, small ambition. I have always wanted to have my life being owned by me and not by others lording a minuscule paycheck over me. Naturally, entrepreneurship became the best vehicle for me to achieve this.

What they don't tell you about being on your own is that this road is fraught with many dangers, disappointments, and struggles. But, when you finally "make it" all of the pain is washed away and your scars are seen as trophies from the battles you have overcome. Trust me when I tell you the feeling is glorious and more than worth it!

That is why I wrote **RULES TO THE GAME**. To help you on your journey towards success and hopefully shield you from some of the mistakes I and others have made so you can benefit and move forward successfully. After all, a wise man learns from the mistakes of others.

What is The Game? The Game is the moniker of the arena where one struggles to succeed by any means necessary. In this book, we will be exploring the ins and outs of The Game and the best ways to navigate it. Although the basis of this book will be from the perspective of the music industry, the lessons gleaned here can be applied to business, life and entrepreneurs as a whole. Your journey will be unique to you and there is no one way to reach the summit of success. These Rules will help you along the way and as such will be a gold mine to you. Happy hustling!

IN THE BEGINNING

My journey started in the summer after 4th grade when I opened my first business – a lemonade and popsicle stand in my apartment complex with my brother, Marcus. When my parents got divorced again in 6th grade, I realized that even though my parents still loved me and will take care of the basics, in order for me to have my own, I had to get it myself. So, I began hustling.

I started with selling Coke cans I "found" in the storage room at my school. Then I moved up to selling candy in 7th grade. In 8th & 9th grade, I was exchanging video game play on my handheld units I got during Christmas (thanks Mom!) for quarters. By 10th grade at just 14 years old, I landed my first W-2 (federally taxed) job at Putt-Putt Golf & Games as the mascot, Buster Ball. My assignment was to make appearances at birthday parties and promo setups along with waving on the side of the road at passing cars in the hot Jacksonville sun.

For me, it was a blessing. I learned how to operate a small business first hand, got paid to play video games and I was responsible for clean up duties, food prep/service, running birthday parties and selling golf tickets (of which, I was the number one salesperson). This is how I was able to pay for all of my music, save up for a car and help finance my way to go to Russia and the Baltic States as an exchange student that summer. (Side note, overseas is when I learned that music, especially hip-hop music is global. I heard rappers in Russian and they had bootleg Dr. Dre's "The Chronic" album on sale in the streets). Additionally, I filed a report for the Jacksonville CBS-TV affiliate about my travels that were broadcast live on air.

During this time, I was blessed to have Mrs. Force as my mentor and favorite teacher. I was the first student to complete the business, law and finance magnet programs simultaneously during my tenure at Wolfson High School. Along with competing in city wide mock law trials, she helped guide me on the right path as my coach in DECA - a competitive business program. I was the first student from my school to win at the regional, state and national levels which allowed me to travel to St. Louis, Detroit and Canada to bring home victory medals two years in a row!

Unfortunately, Putt-Putt closed my senior year of high school, but it made way for the owners to build Adventure Landing the summer before I left to attend Florida State University (#GoNoles). Think of it as a mini-theme park near the beach with go karts, mini-golf, arcade, batting cages and a water park they added the following summer (I helped build that as well when I drove a Bobcat bulldozer for the first time). But, the biggest draw was the pirate themed laser tag arena complete with a huge wooden pirate ship in the lobby to attract players. I was a part of the first pirate crew to run laser tag (fyi, I got the high score on the first game by discovering Sniper's Point!). It was a great opportunity where I got to engage with guests in character during the briefings before the games.

It is also where I experienced getting fired for the first time (although during my journey it wouldn't be the last..lol). I ran afoul of management politics and I learned that even if you are good at your job, if management wants you gone, it's a wrap. But, the crew loved me and gave me a great swashbuckling send off to the tune of "Gangsta Lean" by D.R.S., which was popular at the time.

THE INTERNSHIP OF A LIFETIME

Steve Jobs (founder, Apple Computers) once spoke about dots in your life that connect the large picture of your path. Let me tell you about one of these pivotal dots for me. During my sophomore year at FSU, I was contemplating what I wanted to do with my future career when divine intervention took place and I took advantage. A former artist and current classmate named Cool V gave a speech about his trials and successes as an artist. Sensing destiny in my hands, I asked afterwards if he knew anyone in town that provided an internship in the music industry. It was time to get serious about my career path and I figured it was a great way to match my two loves, business and music.

He put me in contact with TJ Chapman and I landed a 14 year internship at TJ's DJs Record Pool that changed my life. To be clear, a record pool is a collection of DJs that pay a pool director a flat monthly fee in order to collect 12" promo vinyl records direct from the record labels. In the days before downloads, one 12" record could cost anywhere between $4-$10 per song in the store and a DJ that is nice on his Technics 1200s would need doubles. Plus, the store would not always have the exclusives or first rights timing that pools received. And a good DJ prided themselves on always having the best records first. As a result, going through the stores to get music could get very expensive and time consuming, so the pools worked out to be a bargain for the DJs. In exchange, they were required to provide feedback on those records to the labels so they can use it for their marketing and promo campaigns.

Beginning with humble roots from a two bedroom townhouse serving as the office, I began by putting up records for various DJs around town and shipping to those out of town. I was now working with DJs such as Lil Jon (multi-platinum producer/artist, creator of Crunk!!!), Smurf (aka Mr. Collipark, multi-platinum producer for Ying Yang Twins, David Banner, Soulja Boy), Magic Mike (first DJ to have a platinum album), Will Packer (top movie director & producer, "Stomp The Yard," "Takers," "Think Like A Man" & many more), and NYCE (aka Needlz, Grammy Award winning producer for Bruno Mars, 50 Cent and many more). Plus local legends such as Demp (Celebrity DJ x founder, Demp Week), Chuck (the silent Godfather, who also taught me how to mix with vinyl), Saxwell (the Dapper Don – RIP), Dap (PD,

WWLD Blazin' 102.3 - Tallahassee) and Mega Ace who literally opened the doors for me at The Moon – the #1 party spot in Tallahassee.

I didn't get paid monetarily at first but I found the wealth in knowledge. Getting to be the first person around the latest music every day plus making suggestions to the DJs, collecting information, connections and experience was more than enough for me. In fact, I had been doing so well, when TJ first offered to pay me, I asked if he was sure because I was happy to be doing it for free. He already had a gold plaque (500,000 units sold) from his work with the "So So Def's Bass All-Stars" project, so I figured I could learn a great deal from him and eventually attain my own plaque(s) someday. But, I had to take a pause when I came home for the summer.

When I got fired from Adventure Landing, I had my first grown responsibility to take care of, a $264.10 car note due every month. And since my mother co-signed for my car, I couldn't let her take the hit of a repo. So, through a fellow fired former Adventure Landing pirate named Bones, I ended up getting a job at Walmart as a stockman and collecting carts in the sweltering summer sun. One day as I was pushing carts, I don't know if it was the onset of heatstroke, but I had an epiphany. I asked myself, 'is pushing carts really what you want to do with your life? This TJ's DJs thing might be a good move.' Then and there, I made an active decision to see how far we can take it and I'm glad I did.

When I came back to FSU for my junior year, I was all in and never went back home for the summer again. I did everything TJ asked of me and then some. I wasn't even bothered that he brought in someone to, in my eyes, replace me while I was gone for the summer because I knew I was the best for the position. I learned that competition breeds excellence. The DJs I was servicing began to recognize me so I started getting in clubs for free and they respected and played my suggestions for club bangers. Then as I was tasked with creating the feedback charts to provide to the labels, I began making those office connects as well. My competition fell off and suddenly it was just me TJ trusted to handle things while he was away.

Eventually, TJ rewarded my hard work by naming me 'music director' and taking me to my first music conference in Miami, named Impact – the premier industry conference led by the trade magazine of the same name. Coincidentally, that was also the year that the historic Hard Knock Life tour ended its run in Miami at the same time and Def Jam stole the show with its industry showcase. That weekend I saw the whole Def Jam / Hard Knock Life talent roster hit the stage including Jay-Z & the Roc-A-Fella Roster, DMX, an epic Redman & Method Man performance & Ja Rule falling off the stage. I even met Jay-Z, DMX and the Ruff Ryders! I rubbed elbows with legends like the producer, Prince Paul and now all of the DJs and label executives that had previously just been a voice on the phone were now all of my buddies as we hung out. All the parties, shows, networking, and panel discussions had my young excited mind swirling. And to top it off, the conference was at the Fontainebleau, the same hotel they filmed the ice cream scene in "Scarface"!?? — I was sold to The Game for life.

After I came back to the office, I went even harder in the paint. We were on the cusp of innovation by crafting CDs that DJs could play instead of vinyl. In Florida, strip club DJs broke the music and they all played CDs now. So, we went back to Impact the next year in Nashville and had to defend ourselves against those fearful of the next wave. I learned that change is inevitable, roll with it or get run over. Those opponents soon died off because of their lack of vision which put TJ's DJs, newly redubbed TJ's DJs Record & CD Pool in the leadership position for the entire network of record pools throughout the country. This meant that I began speaking on panels at the subsequent annual Impact conferences in Dallas and Orlando. This was a big deal as I was usually the youngest speaker on stage. Amazingly, believe it or not, we were literally laughed at by those in industry power positions just because we were from the South. But, we didn't care because like Andre 3000 championed, "we from the South, and we got something to say!" We went from forcing our way to the industry table to now becoming the head of it.

Along with TJ's DJs we grew into Wildstyle Music & More, a music retail store complete with label, studio and clothing store (s/o Willie "White Shoe" Williams). Since I was responsible for the music store and the growing company as a whole, I had to handle employees (hiring & firing), payroll, marketing, product ordering and reporting to Soundscan. Soundscan is the computer tracking tabulation system that accounts for sales. Whenever an album goes gold (500,000 sales) or platinum (1 million), it is based off of Soundscan numbers. This means that labels place a high priority with marketing dollars and campaigns on stores that report friendly numbers. Between the first location on Capital Circle, two in the flea markets and the clothing store in the Tallahassee Mall, we had four reporting stores in Tallahassee and the labels loved us! We were the only reporting location between Jacksonville, Orlando, Atlanta and New Orleans. As such, they sent money for ad space, artists for in-stores, and all the promo materials we could handle.

As it happened, since it was also the leading industry trade magazine, Impact spun off into the retail charting. I was placed on the Impact Dream Team retail conference call (s/o Tenny Ellison for the opportunity) with all of the leading retailers around the country including industry legends like George Daniels in Chicago that launched R. Kelly, VIP Records that sparked Snoop Dogg (featured in his "What's My Name?" video) and Gary Hozenthal in New Orleans (who moved alot of Cash Money units) and more. In fact, this conference call is how I ended up at the 1st BET Awards in Las Vegas. Beyond it being the first, the award show became historic when Whitney Houston declared Bobby Brown to be "the King of R&B."

Now with all of the connects at labels, whenever artists came through town to promote I was getting a check to be their tour guide to take them to all of the radio stations, hot spots, clubs, and hood locales. I took care of artists from Big Oomp Camp (DJ Unk, Hitman Sammy Sam, Intoxicated), Universal Records artists like Something For The People ("My Love Is The Shh") and Dirty ("Hit Da Floe"), No Limit Records (Fiend & others), Fonzworth Bentley

(Diddy x Outkast x Gentleman Extraordinaire) & 50 Cent who at the time was learning "How To Rob" the industry. In addition, we were hired to promote various campaigns such as Kellogg's Cereal and music like "Shawty Swing My Way" by KP & Envyi for not only Tallahassee, but throughout the southeast too. This scratched my other itch of always wanting to travel, and even better, getting paid to.

We also flipped the retail connects to power our upcoming Wildstyle Records album releases by Total Kaos such as "Y2Kaos" and the phenomenal follow up "Black November" featuring the Tallahassee classic, "That's My Dawg." That is until things went haywire when the artist decided to pursue other options and the label folded just when it was about to really take off. We were devastated and it forced us to change gears. I learned that in The Game, when things don't go to plan, you must learn to adapt.

THE MIGHTY OAK BEGINS WITH A SINGLE ACORN

At this point, I'm in my early 20s and as T.I. said it best on "Be Easy," "I'm 22 and a vet in the game / say I'm super cool but a threat at the same time." The next transition became us pivoting and creating the TJ's DJs Record Pool meetings. Little did we realize at the time how impactful they would become.

Our first conference was the Urban Music Conference in Spring 2000 at Florida A&M University. It was geared towards college students interested in joining the industry. Tony Mercedes (exec producer, "Who Dat Is (Baby Daddy)" was up for a Grammy, Lil Jon explained the secret to a hit record as he transitioned full time into a producer, plus we had the managers of the Violator All-Stars (Fat Joe, Missy, Busta Rhymes & others) and a ton of other talent come to speak to the students. It had its bugs, but overall the event was a great success. So, when it became time to fulfill our duties as a record pool and start having periodic meetings, we folded the label and focused on the conferences and the Wildstyle stores.

In Fall 2001, the first record pool meeting was held in the side room at The Moon called The Silver Moon Lounge and all that were there fit into one picture. It was quaint but effective. DJs got a chance to meet artists, labels got direct access to the DJs and we provided a forum to discuss issues and upcoming industry trends. It went so well we decided to do it again the next quarter and the quarter after that and so on from 2001-2010. I was shocked and thrilled when Big Gipp from Goodie Mob came, then David Banner fresh from his studio van wearing the famous red Mississippi jacket promoting his solo campaign before the Universal deal, then Nappy Headz featuring the future T-Pain, followed by Pretty Ricky as independent artists and many more to follow.

Soon, we had hundreds of people coming. Then it turned into thousands. Artists like Rick Ross, Lil Scrappy, Trillville and Plies that were once unknowns when they came through the now re-titled, TJ's DJs Tastemakers Only DJ/Music Conference, became superstars and credited us for the break that they needed. BET's "Rap City" and "106 & Park" were steadily playing artists on their Top 10 that were once regulars at our conference and by 2003-04, the Southern music scene exploded. And we were on the forefront of the wave.

I was responsible for the event coordination and marketing/sales for the conferences. Before we knew it, we were selling out The Moon as a private event before they opened the doors for the party that night. Word was, you had to come to the TJ's DJs Tastemakers conferences if you had any shot of being able to make it. In fact, our website, tjsdjs.com was garnering 20 million hits per month thanks in part to the message boards. Label heads like Smurf at ColliPark would use the site to launch new projects like Ying Yang Twins "Wait" resulting in having a hit record by going viral on the boards. Additionally, we parlayed many up and comers to new record deals like T-Pain, Tampa Tony, Rated R, Huey, Grind Mode and so many others. Now established stars were not only coming to promote their new projects like Chilli from TLC, Q from 112, Tiny from Xscape, T.I., Pastor Troy, Too $hort, and Young Joc but they would hit the stage and sometimes pay us for the privilege.

We outgrew The Moon and partnered with OZONE Magazine to create The Annual Tastemakers Only / OZONE Awards (TOA's). We then took over Orlando in '06 with Lil Wayne & Trina, Miami in '07 with Ludacris, UGK & Jeezy and Houston in '08 with Geto Boys, J Prince & Rap-A-Lot. In a few consistent years, we went from everyone fitting in one picture to tens of thousands of the top industry execs, DJs, media outlets, artists, and labels coming to our event featuring hundreds of volunteers, $500,000 budgets, sold out host hotels and negotiating rebroadcast rights deals with MTV. Artists that I admired while growing up like Big Boi (Outkast) and Mya were now my guests. Once excited to attend an industry conference, we now became the leading conference of the industry. Coming from such humble beginnings it felt great being on top of the world, especially after the initial resistance of the powers that be in the industry. You just never know where one idea and consistency will take you.

Additionally, my writing talent was taking off too. I became a professional bio writer for artists (thanks C. Wakeley & BloodRaw for my first opportunity), wrote music reviews, published feedback charts and created the weekly TJ's DJs Newsletter that utilized the new tech at the time of email lists to directly influence and report what was happening in the Southeast. I interviewed a ton of executives and artists such as Wayne Wonder, T.I., Swizz Beatz, and Mike Jones that were published in The Source, Vibe, OZONE, Down and countless others. I was once even quoted on BET's "106 & Park" from a bio I wrote for B.o.B!

Speaking of, TJ found B.o.B, his next diamond in the rough, just after breaking T-Pain and as the industry collapsed under the weight of the new internet movement. Around this time, the advent of social media and file sharing revolutionized how people obtain and share music. Now instead of being forced to buy CDs at $10-20 each, you could download your favorite song or even the whole album for free. Plus, artists had a direct connection through Myspace to build their own following. The industry took a while to adapt and reacted very poorly initially.

First, labels started criminalizing DJs who made mixtapes using the promo material they received from the labels. Which made us very nervous passing out the vinyl & CDs they sent to us. It felt like a form of entrapment. Especially when famous mixtape DJs such as Drama were catching federal cases as "bootleggers." Then the labels sued all of the file sharing systems beginning with Napster and Limewire along with the people that downloaded the materials. Eventually they realized that they had to create a new business model so they created 360 deals to find new ways to capitalize on artist money and they started licensing music for file sharing services such as iTunes, Tidal, and others. What all of this meant for us at the time was that the big budget promo gravy train had dried up.

The Wildstyle stores couldn't maintain a proper profit margin without the promo dollars. Combine that with people now buying music sparingly, if at all, forced the stores to close. The artists didn't have to come to conferences to get information or connections due to the new social media wave of Myspace, Facebook and Twitter, so they dried up too. And since DJs didn't have to play vinyl any longer, they downloaded an mp3 and played that on their new Serato Scratch. The record pool was now obsolete.

TJ has always been good about discovering new trends musically and technologically. So, when he discovered B.o.B as a teenager at a showcase in Atlanta, he believed with everything possible that he was to be the next star. Since everything else was pivoting once again, it became time to adapt. We put everything we had including the last drop of cash oil into the B.o.B machine with blind faith hoping that it would pay off. It took a few years, but with 5 Grammy nominations, co-launching Bruno Mars, and 40 million units sold later, TJ proved to be correct and once again silenced the naysayers.

Before that success, waiting on B.o.B to take off and times becoming tight in the meantime, I channeled my creative energies with a sports/talk show entitled "The 2 Minute Warning" with my partner Shane "The Insane" Garner. He made his bones as the DJ behind Bigga Rankins and Cool Runnings – Jacksonville musical legends. Being a huge sports fan and of the Jaguars in particular, Shane and I created the show as a way for us to blend our two passions, sports and music. It started small, but week after week our little podcast that could grew into an outlet that had guest athletes such as world boxing champ, Winky Wright and 2x Super Bowl winner Vince Wilfork (who was kind enough to invite me, my Pops and my brother to watch a game at Foxboro Stadium in the skybox when they played the Jags). We had artists like Young Cash (Nappy Boy Ent / Universal Records) bringing us their music first to debut. And by the time we worked up to having our show on commercial radio, we were even sponsored by The Florida Times-Union, McDonald's and Wing Zone. Plus, NFL and NBA athletes that started new labels hired me to help them consult their campaigns. And thus, my company 24K Konsulting was born to help others help themselves.

GETTING GROWN

Over time I became a decorated industry vet and now, the next generation looked to me for advice and guidance so I created an educational mixtape series, the "Money Making Mixtape" featuring guest hosts such as Too $hort and Wendy Day (the architect of Cash Money's $30 million deal, David Banner's $10 million deal & discovered Eminem) to help break down the industry and I went on the road speaking on panels and schools. (Special thanks to Glenn Jr. for recording, K Grace for the artwork and Chazmen / Brashaad for always having the T.Y.M.E. - Transforming Your Mind & Energy to give back!)

In 2011 after all of the successes, disappointments and opportunities I felt it was time for me to spread my wings and leave the TJ's DJs nest. Now in my early 30s, I was no longer the wide-eyed kid happy to be there, I was grown and it was time for me to fly solo and build my own legacy. I resigned as Vice President of the now fully evolved music marketing company, TJ's DJs, Inc. Shortly after, I was hired by Akon (CEO/artist/producer/city builder) to be on a promo campaign as a great way to get started on my solo career. Thankfully, he remembered me for being one of the first to write a positive review in OZONE Magazine for his debut album, "Trouble."

Akon, fresh from his multi-platinum success as a solo artist and producer of Jeezy, Gwen Stefani and others, then as the executive producer with T-Pain and Lady Gaga, he was now looking to promote his next artist, Money Jay on his label Konvict Muzik.

I was recruited to handle the Florida arm of the national campaign as a part of a team of industry heavyweights for this project. I hired my public speaking partner, Brashaad Mayweather (now an accomplished actor and we hit the road, 10 Florida cities in 11 days. I had to show up and show out because this was my opportunity to shine. We passed out thousands of flyers to strangers, serviced every DJ, and put up a poster in every hood spot throughout Florida. We did such a great job that Akon thanked me personally and asked me to go on a bigger run. So, this time I put together a promo run by myself of 19 cities over 21 days in 4 states culminating in New Orleans for July 4 weekend with the Essence Festival. I felt wonderful when I got my check while sitting on a beach during the campaign.

I was so proud of the work I put in. Unfortunately, Money Jay didn't take off and Akon dropped the project and most directly, I lost my biggest client. But, that's how The Game goes. I was able to sparingly pick up a few promo projects however, they barely scratched the surface of my monthly bills. After the Akon money dried up and I didn't have any other paying prospects, I had to do the most embarrassing thing an entertainment executive could do, get a job outside of the industry. However, in life, one does what one must.

THE TRANSITION

This time of my life I consider to be called The Transition. I had to learn how to grow from being high on the horse in The Game to being humbled so I could re-learn how to stand on my own two feet. Starting fresh and working my way from the bottom to create a fantastic bounce back was the new mission.

I answered an ad on Craigslist that fit what I was looking for; a sales job with variable hours that gets paid regardless of making a sale. Sounded like a win-win. But when I went in for the interview, come to find out it was for selling Cutco knives. I admit I was disappointed and almost walked out. My brother told me that it was time for me to tighten up, so I did. I made an active decision to understand that I was there for a reason. I decided to buckle down, handle my biz, learn from it and keep moving forward. And I am so grateful that I did because it became another major dot in my life.

I was blessed to work on the team under the leadership of Tyler Tarr. He put me onto so much salesmanship game and marketing techniques (we'll discuss some of them later in this book). Combined with my hunger and experience I quickly was moving many more units than the other sales people. I rocketed to Top 10 salesman every week and got a seat at the inner office circle. I realized that Cutco was making millionaires out of those that really put in work. I didn't have any better options so I did everything I could to become one of them. As I moved more units, I made more money and it became easier. Plus on a personal note, I met a great love of my life through the program when I needed her the most to help me through the storm (thanks Mahogani*, you're the bestest!). I learned that a strong support system is necessary for your best chance to succeed.

But, as with all sales jobs, you have hot and cold streaks. Some where you can't do any wrong and every call is a sale and also others when you do everything right and can't catch a break. The inconsistency was becoming a financial problem.

At the same time, I kept a foot in The Game by writing an occasional bio, consulting on an indie project or two, but nothing big really panned out. This is also when I realized that if you are not of service to people and are out of sight, you are out of mind. My phone didn't ring nearly as much as it once did and there were only a handful of people out of the thousands that I worked with that actually called and did a wellness check on me during this Transition.

During this time, and I will be 1,000% with you, like my Jaguars, I saw few wins and suffered significant losses, dark days and some might say a deep depression. I lost my mother, step-brother (s/o Big Rube!) and almost my father too. The only money I could generate was by selling blood or through odd jobs on Craigslist. I got turned down for job opportunities in the corporate world, state jobs, a position as an apartment leasing manager, the Jaguars, and even Target. I could only find work at Advanced Auto Parts (until I got fired on my day off) and later Poker's Print Shop in the hood (thanks Reggie!).

I was beyond broke and a week from losing my house to foreclosure which by the way, just sprung a water heater leak I couldn't afford to fix. I was in credit card debt beyond hope and forget about having a positive credit score for a loan. My heat / ac was broken in my house for many years. And my car died so the bus route and walking were my only mobile options. But, something in me kept moving forward. The classic movie, "Galaxy Quest" taught me, "never give up, never surrender."

David Banner, Julia Beverly (founder, OZONE Magazine), DJ Scorpio (Atlanta), Brother Joe, Renee, White Shoe, DJ Debonair, Garris, Kaos and a handful of others occasionally reached out to check on me. My family did what they could (shout out to Marcus, Mom, Pops, Margo & Mahogani* – I love you all!) to be there for me. However, family can only support a grown man so much. DJ Dap & Butch, invited me out into nature to help me heal through fishing. But, it was DJ Chuck that helped me stay on the industry

20

track. As I was going through this dark period, I am grateful to him because as a photographer for the local paper, The Tallahassee Democrat, he would invite me out to various events and offered advice that saved my sanity more often than he realized.

On one such occasion, I ran into Ms. Jackie Bennett who was the Momager (Mom/Manager of DJ Lil Boy. Since he was on the road as T-Pain's official DJ, we had lost touch. Before then he was a young kid soaking up every ounce of game from us at the TJ's DJs office. He was a professional DJ in elementary school, had an official business by middle school and by high school, ran the teen party scene in Tally. When he graduated, he hit the road with T-Pain as "I'm Sprung" took off and he had been running around the world for the next 10 years.

Ms. Jackie informed me that Lil Boy was getting tired of the road life and wanted to come home to re-center himself. She explained that she is a bit older now and doesn't have the time or energy to devote to this next phase. She remembered how well I handled business at TJ's DJs and said she would be proud to have her son work with me because I would treat him fairly and handle things correctly. I looked at this opportunity as a great honor. There are few things in life Ms. Jackie played with and none of them were about her son.

Now, here is the other blessing. Remember how I told you how the Cutco inconsistency was becoming a problem? Well, I happened to run into a friend from high school named Jules by reconnecting through Cutco. I told him about what was going on and he put me on to his other gig, US Airways (and later American Airlines when they merged. In exchange for checking people in, slinging bags, cleaning the planes at night and working outside no matter the weather, I received a steady check and free flights anywhere US Airways / American flies in the US and I just pay the taxes on international flights. Bet!

As such, I took full advantage and began to travel the world like Caine in the TV show, "Kung-Fu." I visited longtime friends and family in New York, Phoenix and Boston. I set up client bases in Philly, Atlanta, Tampa and Miami. I flew to London for the Olympics. I went to SXSW with FLX (filmmaker for Revolt) where I met Snoop plus saw Kendrick Lamar tell everyone not to "Kill My Vibe" and was one of the first to get a Beats Pill. I would even fly to Jacksonville for the Jags games, normally a 2 hour drive, just because I could. I put my parents on my roster so they could fly too. I soaked up some sun and culture on several Caribbean islands. I took my brother to backpack in Europe on his first ever 1st class international flight. We went to Wimbledon and saw Serena Williams play, climbed the steps of the Eiffel Tower before having lunch in its shadow, gave Mona Lisa the eye, and we hit the Red Light District in Amsterdam. We've sung "Sweet Caroline" at the top of our lungs on the Green Monster at Fenway Park. And most historically, we were in the front row of Outkast's historic last show in Atlanta and at the Rose Bowl to watch Florida State win a championship ring in person!

Just walking through the airports was an adventure because you never know who you will run into. I met Harry Belafonte, Bobby Bowden, Gene Deckerhoff, Jameis Winston, Biz Markie, Michael Eric Dyson, Michael Madsen, Ben Crump, Tim Tebow and even TJ on occasion. I even once saved the FSU cheerleaders when they got stuck in Tally and got them on a plane to the Syracuse game on time! It was a great run at the airlines until I got fired for politics and insubordination. Although the benefits were great, micromanagement and I don't get along very well so, it was time for the next chapter of my life.

Now back to DJ Lil Boy. After the meeting with his mother, he and I connected and he invited me to the next T-Pain show at the House of Blues in Houston. Courtesy of one of my last airline flights, I saw his energy on stage and how he commanded the show by outshining T-Pain. In that moment, my next dot was revealed as I was convinced DJ Lil Boy was a star. I thought, "this is what TJ must have felt when he found B.o.B."

Lil Boy and I spoke about future plans and what we both wanted to do and get out of this. Next thing I know, I now have a major client and we hit the road completing his obligations. First stop was the One Spark Festival in Jacksonville. It is a crowd funded tech event attended by over 100,000 people that DJ Lil Boy was the host DJ for. I lined up after party gigs for him, promoted his festival mixtape, handled the business and we didn't stop moving for 3 straight days! We hustled our first check together, gained a mutual respect and built a friendship as well that has allowed us to be on and popping ever since!

We created annual events such as S.A.B Fest (Students Against Bullying Festival) that partners media outlets, local businesses along with public speakers such as the Leon County Sherriff's Office, the Mayor of Tallahassee and US Congressman Al Lawson with the Leon County School board to produce concerts with a purpose featuring talents such as Ayo & Teo ("Rolex"), 69 Boyz, and Koly P (Lil Boosie's protégé) to combat the plague of bullying in our schools. We have created talent showcases to utilize the M.E.A.P (Music Entrepreneur & Arts Program) that teaches kids how to create a business using their talents and then showcasing them on stage at the "Hype of the City" events. I have booked talent for FSU, Blazin' 102.3's Birthday Bash and DJ Lil Boy's overseas shows. Plus, we created several businesses including United Trophies & Awards and The Venue, a multi-purpose facility that has now grown to be the #1 spot in Tally.

Additionally, I do speaking engagements and mentor high school students via Take Stock In Children at Tallahassee Community College. It is a program for 1st generation low income students that upon completion and graduation, they earn a scholarship to attend TCC.

I have even been on TV as the expert reporter for three episodes of TVOne's "Fatal Attraction."

Upon reflection, I will say that I have transcended my Transition period and now I am in one of New Growth. I am blessed to have survived my trials, bounced back and have been found to remain standing while always moving forward because tough times don't always last, but tough people do. I am eagerly anticipating life as it unfolds into additional exciting opportunities. In the meantime, please use the lessons that I have acquired to help you on your journey. Thank you, most sincerely for taking the time to read this. Take what you feel, apply it as you need and pass the knowledge to the next one who may need it.

If you have any additional questions, follow ups or would like to book me to come speak at a school / university, panel or function near you, please feel free to reach out via Instagram - @KeithK926 or @RulesToTheGame.

With Love Always,

Keith Kennedy
keith@rulestothegame.com
www.rulestothegame.com

Hugs From The Grand Canyon

* * *

50 Cent (l) & Keith (r)

(l-r) Keith, TJ, B.o.B, JB & B Rich

Brothers In Paris

Wildstyle & TJ's DJs Crew

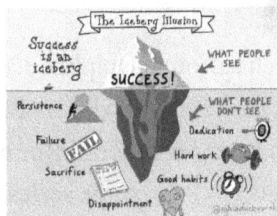

3

WITH A LITTLE HELP FROM MY FRIENDS

"And I can't help the poor if I'm one of them / So I got rich and gave back to me that's the win, win"
JAY-Z - *"Moment of Clarity"*

* * *

A special thank you goes out to the following Tastemakers for their exceptional knowledge that is interspersed within these pages. I am blessed to have you for this project and even more importantly, that I am able to call you my friends.

BIGGA RANKIN

By helping to break artists such as Young Dolph, Lucci, Gotti, Juvenile, Boosie & Webbie, Pastor Troy, Dirty, Rick Ross, and Plies - Bigga Rankin has achieved legendary status as a DJ and founder of Cool Runnings, the DJ crew from Jacksonville. Now through his RNR Mixtape series and as the head A&R of

T.I.G. Records, Bigga is always looking to develop the next wave of talent.

"My blessings come from believing in God" and "you have to have great work ethics – no excuses!"

Instagram - @biggarankin00

DJ DAP

In addition to being a fan favorite during his afternoon drive time slot, as Program Director for WWLD – Blazin' 102.3 FM in Tallahassee, Larry "DJ Dap" Dunlap has led the station to the unprecedented status of being #1 in the market.

"Focus on your craft, that's the only way you get better."

Instagram - @djdap
www.djdap.com

DJ DEMP

Starting his career in Tallahassee, DJ Demp has grown to become a world class celebrity DJ with appearances on BET and MTV plus travelling as the road DJ for Juvenile, Lil Flip, Trick, Trina, Luke, David Banner & Ghost Town DJs ("My Boo"). But, his annual Demp Week, now in its 23rd year, has earned a proclamation from the mayor of Tallahassee for inviting stars such as Future, Young Jeezy, 8Ball & MJG and so many more to his hometown.

"Stay blessed, stay positive, keep your head up, stay focused, stay humble, stay grounded – don't get the big head cuz at some point it will pop. Don't never get too big to mingle and shake hands or isolate yourself cuz they are the same ones you may need to get where you at."

Instagram - @djdemp

DJ LIL BOY

Starting at age 10, DJ Lil Boy has taken his craft seriously as a profession by creating Lil Boy Productions. Today, it has taken him around the world as T-Pain's road DJ that has supplied 4 passports, a lifetime of experiences and provided the opportunities to launch businesses such as The Venue, a multi-purpose facility, United Trophies & Awards and a studio along with being the #1 rated DJ on the #1 station in Tallahassee, Blazin' 102.3.

"Don't listen to anybody, listen to yourself and you gotta stay consistent."

Instagram - @djlilboy

DJ PRINCESS CUT

DJ Princess Cut aka Sweetbox Jones has been spinning for over 15 years. In that time she has developed into a producer, designer, US Hip-Hop ambassador, world traveler, DJ for Hot 107.9 WHTA – ATL and Hoodrich – Uncut Radio. Plus, she is a professional personality and corporate DJ with Neiman Marcus and owns a DJ school – ScratchOutLoud.com that focuses on teaching the art of turntablism with vinyl. And she is the road DJ for The-Dream, Outlawz, Goodie Mob and Oprah.

"Stay positive…practice hard…get into it, be passionate about it, even if it is discouraging…if you fall down, get back up. Even if you have heard it before, it is what it is. Trust your instincts. Respect the ones that have come before you."

Instagram - @djprincesscut

E. MACKEY

E. Mackey is the consummate hustler and entrepreneur. He is nice with photography, an accomplished author and an excellent graphic designer (in fact, he designed this book's cover and logo). As the founder of his latest project, Blvck Spades, he is putting a new urban face on playing cards. Plus, he is a documentarian focusing on shedding light on racial divides as a way to bring us together.

"You can endure but you have to be resilient. You have to believe in your dream. You have to believe in your brand, value that and keep going."

info@blvckspades.com
Instagram - @blvckspades
www.facebook.com/blvckspades

JAHMAL BESLEY

"Jah" is a graphic artist that has parlayed his talent into owning Empire Tattooz for the past 12 years. He has also earned the reputation of a chess master as well as wise street philosopher.

"If you have an idea, don't wait. Plan it out and execute it. Don't be good at it, be great at it. 'No' is not a word I accept, 'can't' is not one I tolerate. Always be comfortable in what you do and protect yourself."

Instagram - @whasmuname

JULIA BEVERLY

Most people know Julia from her days as the publisher and editor of OZONE Magazine. Since that time, she continues being a photojournalist, has gone on to publish two books about Pimp C & J Prince, created Agency Twelve for talent booking, dabbles in real estate and became a biking / hiking world traveler one country mile at a time.

"I never knew taking pictures in the club at 19 [years old] would lead to a career that would take me around the world to have a lot of great experiences through hip-hop. If you can stick with it through passion and work ethic to produce multiple sources of income, you can definitely find a way to make it work."

Instagram - @juliabeverly

KINGPIN aka RAP JUGGERNAUT

This promotional machine represents Promo Vatican, Core DJs, Team Bigga Rankin, and Coast 2 Coast DJs among others. His devotion to getting the word out is seconded only by the importance he places on his relationships.

"Grind like nobody owes you nothing cuz at the end of the day, nobody gives a f*ck!"

Instagram - @rapjuggernaut

KRISTIN DUNGEE

Kristin aka Kakekini is an entrepreneur that has dedicated her life to strengthening "her muscle to hustle." After securing her BS Degree in Multi-National Business Operations at Florida State University, she has gone on to become an NFL cheerleader with the Miami Dolphins & NY Jets, artist, author, web & graphic designer, dancer, nutritionist and found time to become a certified personal trainer including a certification in pilates.

"If you want to be successful at anything having a mentor really does help. They can help encourage you on your path."

Instagram - @kakekini

MARCUS KENNEDY

After earning an Engineering Degree from Florida State, Marcus worked for Kraft Foods and then moved on to become the GM of the Gaming & E-Sports division at Intel. Along the way, he earned a Master's Degree at Babson College, the number one school for entrepreneurial ventures in the world. He has bought and sold businesses, developed real estate and on the financial side received a Series 7 & Series 65 to give financial advice. Plus, he has a Lean Six Sigma Black Belt which means he knows how to make things more efficient.

"Remember cash flow is king whether you are a really big corporation or you are a smaller entrepreneur. Always know where your money is going, figure out what you want to do with it and build towards your dream."

Contact: info@rulestothegame.com

OG MAGNUM

OG Magnum has lived a colorful life filled with stories for days. But, this student of the world has brought a new dimension by becoming an American Meme through appearances in videos by Plies and other hip-hop stars. He is also a social media influencer, promoter, advocate and motivational speaker. Plus, as President & CEO of the Florida Custom Car Association, he fights to make sure car enthusiasts can enjoy their hobby without undue prosecution.

"Be aware, be patient, have passion, get educated and get your paperwork squared away."

Instagram - @og.magnum
www.ogmagnum.com

THRILL DA PLAYA

As a member of the world famous, 69 Boyz, Thrill is responsible for selling over 35 million units over his career. Still performing and recording, Thrill's musical journey has been one of highs and lows but he is always there to rock a show!

"It's a journey. Without the journey, you have no stories to tell and your life is boring. You gotta live your life. Good comes with the bad, water comes with the wet. The good times are the celebration. The tribulations are the things you remember and hold onto the most because these are the things that make you look and see what faith has brought you through."

Instagram - @thrilldaplaya

TJ CHAPMAN

This entertainment mogul has orchestrated many deals including being instrumental in getting T-Pain and B.o.B signed among others. Plus, he has been the owner of a studio, music and clothing stores and founded TJ's DJs – a record pool that has grown into a highly influential music marketing company. It spawned the TJ's DJs Tastemakers Only DJ/Music Conferences that were the leading provider of industry knowledge and connections as well as breaking numerous acts from Rick Ross, Plies, Pretty Ricky, David Banner and so many more. Today, TJ is the manager for B.o.B, Trap Beckham, former manager of K Camp and creator of @FreeMusicReviewTV.

"It's all about the relationships, don't be afraid to try. Some people get so caught up in being afraid to fail that they don't even try. You only miss the shots you don't take."

Instagram - @tjsdjs

WENDY DAY

Wendy Day is the founder of the Rap Coalition. It is an organization designed to help artists out of bad deals and provides information to help them find better ones. She has put massive deals together including the ones for Cash Money, No Limit, David Banner and Eminem. Currently, she has a youtube channel to help get the word out about understanding The Game.

"Learn as much as you can about the business. It appears easy from the outside looking in and it's not."

Instagram - @rapcoalition
www.youtube.com/thisiswendyday

UNCLE HEAD

Uncle Head has been filling dance floors as a member of the 90s seminal group Splack Pack for nearly 3 decades. Mr. "Scrub Da Ground / Shake Dat A$$ / Let Me See You Work It" created his own label, Bottom Lyne Records to keep dropping new music that will have his fans dancing for many years to come.

"You gotta invest your money in something other than music. You gotta work. There's no sleep. I only get 3-4 hours of sleep because I'm constantly on the grind, working. Ain't no vacation time."

Instagram - @unclehead72

ZAKIYA ALTA LEE

After spending four glorious years as a dancer for the NBA's Atlanta Hawks, Zakiya decided to help the next generation of hopefuls by founding Z Pro Prep to help you get on a professional team. Besides learning the techniques to be great dancers, her graduates grace sidelines in the NBA and the NFL blessed with knowledge of self as a result of the positive energy from her camps.

"You are enough. Everything you need to succeed, you have in you right now. In this moment, you have everything you need to accomplish every goal that God has put you on this Earth to accomplish."

Instagram - @z_proprep

* * *

NOTES TO SELF // TODAY I LEARNED ... // MY NEXT STEP IS ...

4

DON'T BE SCURRED — LEAP OF FAITH

"For we walk by faith, not by sight."
THE BIBLE (*2 Corinthians 5:7*)

===

"The journey of a thousand miles must begin with a single step."
LAO TZU (*Founder, Taoism*)

===

"The only way to do great work is to love what you do."
STEVE JOBS (*Founder, Apple Computers*)

===

"My Umi said shine your light on the world / Shine your light for the world to see"
MOS DEF - *"Umi Says"*

* * *

It is commendable that you are taking the time to make difficult changes in your life to achieve your greatness. Take time to appreciate that this is no easy task. Too often in life, we take the path of least resistance. Then we wonder why we feel as though our life is out of control or in an irreversible rut. We must make the active decision to take control of our lives. Otherwise, one day you will realize you are in a place you did not intend because you were adrift due to a lack of directed action. Yes, there will be hazards along the way and it will be difficult, but the satisfaction of achieving your end game goals will far outweigh the hardships you may endure.

But first things first, you must take that leap. It is scary to take a step forward without knowing what will happen next. Here is the secret, you already know where you will end up. You have the vision in your mind. You can see yourself at life's finish line having lived the life you have always wanted. Therefore, if you know it will happen, all you have to do is take the first steps toward it and handle everything in between. You can do it!

It is natural to want to feel safe and protected. Millions of years of evolution have designed us to take the safe route whenever possible. But, if we always did the safe thing, we never would have left the caves or used fire as a tool. The professional equivalent of staying in a cave is accepting a 9-5 job with security and a stable check. For some, that is all one needs in life. It is great at first until you begin to realize that you are not fulfilling your true calling or making the maximum use of your talents. For the entrepreneur, this is a recipe for misery.

It took my mother being fired for being sexually harassed and me working in a cubicle at the investment company Smith Barney Shearson during my high school 11th grade summer for me to realize that office life was not for me. The highlight of my day was the morning bagel and watching "The Young & The Restless" with the secretary pool during lunch. The rest of the day was filled with mindless tasks, petty disagreements with jealous co-workers and massive amounts of clock watching. The check was great and I did what I was asked to do very well, but it was not worth my sanity.

Eventually, as an entrepreneur these positions will begin to feel confining and restricting to your creativity and natural talents. The steady check generally keeps you just above water where you can keep your lights on and if you save up for a long time, you might be able to do something nice for yourself, but not enough to live the fantastic life you may want to or dream of. You aren't allowed to make too much money and if you need a raise, you have to present your case to a manager that gets paid for keeping costs down and the worker bees buzzing. Of course, the odds are never in your favor. In this case, JOB stands for Just Over Broke.

One day you will look up years down the road and realize that you aren't happy surviving check to check. And even worse, having someone else with a "boss" title is now in control over your destiny. What happens when the company gets downsized? What happens when you can't afford to stay and can't afford to leave? What happens if there is a pandemic and your job no longer exists? How will you take care of yourself or your family? Lorenzo from the movie, "A Bronx Tale" said it best, "the saddest thing in life is wasted talent."

The Game is designed to be difficult as a barrier to entry. But, when you play it right, you will be in control. You will dictate when, how and who you work with. There will be no salary cap except for what you make it to be. Your earning potential is directly tied into your work. It is there for you to take it. But, it begins with that first leap of faith. It will all be worth it when you are doing what you were put on this Earth for – fulfilling your destiny and living your best life on your terms.

Thrill Da Playa has this to say about taking a leap. "Prayer, faith and your belief in God is everything. [It's about] not knowing what's on the other side of the door and to keep pushing. The last time I didn't have the strength, He brought me through. If I can remember the last time, why would I doubt Him this time? Don't quit on your dream."

We all have a super power. One that is unique to just us. It's the one talent or skill that comes easy to you but not so much to others. Some would call it a niche. When you find yours, trust it and max it for all it is worth. That is your ticket to your destiny. Just make sure that you do not decide your niche based on how much money you plan to make. There are plenty of rich miserable people in the world. Find the niche that brings joy to your life and fulfilment, then you will be rich beyond measure in peace of mind and the money will come as a byproduct - if you put in the work.

The Game is often played sight unseen except for the vision you have for yourself. Do not expect others to join you easily. You will be mocked and ridiculed by those that are stuck on their own hamster wheel. Do not give the naysayers any energy. They will not understand because they are worker bees and you are a boss. They are not on your level.

As Jay-Z said on "Boss," "everybody bosses til it's time to pay for the office / til them invoices separate the men from the boys." No worries, when you become successful, they will be the first to congratulate. Even better, they will want to work for you.

Julia Beverly offers this advice, "if you are passionate, stay focused and dedicated, you definitely can make money from [The Game]. I like shooting. Sitting back chilling is not my thing. [I had] a way better situation at OZONE instead of at a 'real magazine.' Nobody called me back at XXL [Magazine], but in the end it forced me to put all of my own energy into my own project and when it comes down to it, ownership is the best deal possible. Of course you have your headaches and liabilities but you can never be fired. It's all about how hard you decide to go with it. I gradually realized that ownership is a better deal for me."

She goes on to say, "OZONE magazine in the beginning was like 'who?' Then when they started recognizing the name, they put me right through. Name recognition is what helped me realize I was on the right track."

TJ Chapman agrees by stating, "People don't believe. You have to be a visionary when they ain't got there yet. If there is something you believe in, you have to stand by your guns. But, you also have to be willing to accept it if it don't happen too, now. I had so many things that I was wrong about, that didn't happen but I learned and eventually got right."

He continues, "I don't know everything, but the sh!t that I know, I know and you can't tell me nothing. [Regarding B.o.B] They didn't get it. [They would say] 'that ain't gonna work,' 'TJ falling off' and now I'm sitting at 40 million sold, bruh! What you saying now, bruh!? You still in the city, I just got back from my 35th country on this rap sh!t."

The great thing about change is that it is never too late. For example, JK Rowling published Harry Potter in her late 30s. Once you make the active decision to do so, direct all of your positive energies into that change and make it happen. Making a change in your life's direction may be akin to turning an oil tanker rather than a jet ski, but take pride in recognizing the need and want to change, then actually doing it.

EXAMPLE OF THE RULE

My leap of faith came when I decided to resign from TJ's DJs, Inc. After 14 years with the company, I felt boxed in and I was no longer growing with the opportunities that excited me when I began. I was conflicted with feelings of loyalty to the company and attempting to discover what was right for me. I had no idea what was I was to do if I were to ever leave the company because it was all I had ever known while working in the entertainment industry. I just knew that the time had come.

To make the decision even more difficult, we were in the midst of a great run with B.o.B who had just been nominated for 5 Grammy's following the success of "The Adventures of Bobby Ray" project. So I said a prayer, shed a tear and listened to my inner spirit telling me it was time to try something new.

The blessing came when word got out that I was now a free agent. I was contacted by Drew, who was directing Akon's next promo project, Money Jay. I was invited to Atlanta to be a part of the conversations in Konvict Muzik's boardroom. Within the next two weeks, I was on the road promoting the project in 10 Florida cities over 11 days. Then I upgraded to another subsequent run of 19 cities over 21 days in 4 states. And to TJ's credit, I later heard that he gave a positive recommendation for me.

The lesson, take the leap. There's no telling where you will end up landing. Wherever it may be, you will be better and stronger as a result.

Another example is Ice Cube. When John Singleton was set to shoot the now classic movie, "Boyz N The Hood," he reached out to NWA be a part of the project and to be in it. Only Ice Cube stepped outside of his comfort zone and accepted the offer. On that set, he caught the acting bug and saw how movies are made. Soon after, he wrote "Friday" which surprised the industry, made millions and became a classic. Now the gangsterest one of them all is a legit Hollywood producer, director and star with "no vaseline." Step outside of your zone, nothing great has been accomplished by being safe.

A final example is DJ Dap. "I was always told I have a voice for radio. Radio is my passion and it was something that I really wanted to do so I kept the faith. DJ Saxwell (RIP) invited me to fill in shifts at 90.5 to get me started. Then when Will Packer left FAMU to go make movies, he picked me out of everybody to take over his slot. Then the Spoon opportunity came along [to join Hot 105 - Tallahassee] that I never thought would happen to me. I thought 'what other great things can happen to me?'" Eventually, Dap kept taking leaps of faith and took advantage of his opportunities to move up the ladder until he now runs the #1 radio station in Tallahassee - WWLD Blazin' 102.3 FM.

The American Meme, OG Magnum concludes by saying this, "I believe this, not just for artists, but for anybody, is that you must leave where you are from. You must go away. Do it earlier in your career, 17, 18, 19, 20s [years of age], you should leave whatever the f*ck you're from. You should go at least 200 miles away and you should be gone for at least a year. You can always come back. It's not going anywhere and if you do come back, no problem. There's no judgment made but and if you come back, you will find how little it has changed over that time. But that year you spent will grow you immensely because it's all about getting out of where you are and uprooting yourself and replanting and learning how to be able to do that. That's real survival."

YOUR MISSION – C.A.N.I – Constant And Never-Ending Improvement

This is a phrase I picked up during my time with Cutco (thanks Tyler & Erin!). The main reason why people become so good at anything is not necessarily because of talent. It is because they work very hard at their craft to become the best at it. Hard work beats talent if talent doesn't work hard. When you focus and take action to becoming better every day, eventually you can only get better. No matter the task or goal; losing weight, writing a novel, or making your business grow – you have to be able to focus on Constant And Never-Ending Improvement in order to increase your acumen. Don't focus on being perfect, be perfect in the attempt.

DJ Dap is a big proponent of this. "You've got to focus on your craft, that's the only way you get better. You have to give 150%. Even when the work day is over, I am still working. I come in when the company doesn't even pay me because I want to be amazing at what I do and be the top guy. You have to push through all of the noise and work hard."

It takes 10,000 hours of work to become a master of your craft. You might as well get started now!

Promo expert Kingpin adds, "it's about sacrificing, trying to get the job done" and never forget that "humility has gone a long way to help me get where I am." In the end though, "if you stay focused and become the best at what you do, you will be able to write your own check."

Thrill Da Playa agrees that you should "do it with humility and not arrogance. Humility is about others, arrogance is about yourself."

* * *

ACTION STEPS / HOMEWORK

1. Decide that right now is when you will change. Not tomorrow, not later, NOW!!

2. Decide what you want that change to look like. What is your end game? Be as specific as possible.

3. Set a reasonable timeline.

4. Hold yourself accountable, forgive yourself for past transgressions and start again if necessary.

5. Keep moving forward. Don't worry if you slip or it takes longer than you anticipate. Just reset, course correct and keep moving forward.

6. Read "Who Moved My Cheese" by Spencer Johnson. It will teach you about adaptability.

WARNING

Be mindful of the instinct to want to go back to something comfortable or your old ways / positions. The Game cannot be won by being in a comfort zone. Resist the urge to go backwards. Know that you will be ok. Embrace the change and keep moving forward. You will soon open so many new opportunities, you will be upset that you didn't make this change sooner.

Additionally, be on the lookout for the naysayer. This is the person in your circle that has no vision so they would rather throw shots at yours. DO NOT EVER tell your full vision to anyone else. They can disrupt your natural flow of positivity by injecting doubt into your vision. Let them see it develop as you grow. Then they will be the first one's to tell you that they knew you would be successful the whole time.

Zakiya Alta Lee offers this word of caution, "people get frustrated because they are trying to get to the next destination too quickly. Once you accomplish all of your goals, your life is over. Don't rush. You have to enjoy the journey because there is one thing that is more important than building a business and that's building the business owner. All of those things are done during the journey. We have seen people get success too quickly and they destroy themselves because they didn't build during the journey."

* * *

NOTES TO SELF // TODAY I LEARNED ... // MY NEXT STEP IS ...

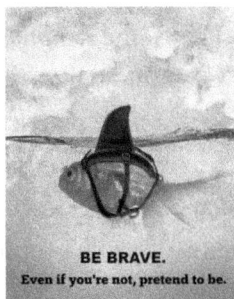

BE BRAVE.
Even if you're not, pretend to be.

42

5

PLAN ACCORDINGLY

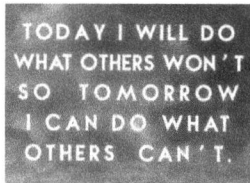

TODAY I WILL DO
WHAT OTHERS WON'T
SO TOMORROW
I CAN DO WHAT
OTHERS CAN'T.

For you to be successful in The Game, you have to have a plan. You must also understand, that not everything will go according to that plan. Don't worry if Plan A doesn't work, you have plan B, C and then 23 more letters in the alphabet to go. The important takeaway is to have at least a general understanding of where you are headed. You can adjust the plan as you go. But, without a proper rudder, you will have no direction and crash on the rocks of life.

As I was pledging to become a member of Alpha Phi Alpha Fraternity, Inc. I was blessed to learn about "The 6 P's." What are they and what do they mean?

THE 6 P'S

PRIOR
PLANNING
PREVENTS
PISS
POOR
PERFORMANCE

Essentially, without a road map of your project before you begin, you will be doomed to yield bad results. There is a certain freedom to winging it and goodness knows I have done my fair share. But, by far the best results have come when there is a specific strategy in mind. If a general goes to war without a plan, the troops are going to have a bad time. If you begin a writing project without an outline, your thoughts will be jumbled and incoherent to the reader plus you may miss details you would have wanted to cover. If an architect builds a structure without the blueprint, it will collapse. Plan your work then work your plan.

Most importantly, DJ Lil Boy explains, "success is not instant. If you make it to the next step and get your goal you have met your success rate. Set long term and short term goals. If I don't put the footwork in, it's just a dream. Any success is a goal that is accomplished." And once you have the plan, DJ Lil Boy advises "stick to the plan, don't get on the playing field and start calling audibles."

When it comes time to execute your plan, Jah Besley suggests that you take "the same energy I put into a 9-5, is the same energy I put into myself. The same energy that you would punch someone else's clock, you have to do it for your own. The worry about being late, sleeping in my truck to make sure

I don't miss a customer, I did it for me. You have to make something of this for all of those that heard 'no.'"

If you come across road blocks because you get a 'no,' Zakiya Alta Lee offers this suggestion, "there are so many more yes's in the world than no's, but you have to go out and find them. Yes's are like Easter Egg hunts. No should give you the energy to keep moving forward to show if you really want it. Perseverance is key, having the drive is important."

And even with the plan, Thrill Da Playa says that the key to "longevity is staying current with times and understanding that timing is everything. You do other things to stay relevant until it's your time again. The streets will tell you what time it is. You can have all the money in the world and drop a project and it won't move. Or if it is your time, you can drop something and it moves naturally. If you are attuned spiritually, you can feel these things. It's a feeling and you can tell when it is right. Don't miss your opportunity."

When you are developing your plan, you must also decide what does success look like? Just as a good general will define the end game in a theatre of war, you must understand what your victory point is. Otherwise, you will be unhappy, stuck going in endless circles like on a hamster wheel, because you will never attain what you do not define.

HOW DO I DEVELOP A PLAN?

Take a moment to work this out as you go. Grab a sheet of paper, use the blank pages of this book or write in the margins. Either way, write these ideas down. Ready? Let's get it!

Know What You Want To Do

Before you begin your project, you must first define what that project is. The more specific, the more effective your plan will be. EXAMPLE - I planned on writing this book.

Work Backwards From Your End Goal

Determine what the end goal is, then create a list of everything necessary to accomplish it from end to start.

EXAMPLE

- I plan to have a book release party complete with a book signing.
- I plan to find a venue, set the date and time for the book release party.
- I plan to have the book published in time for the book release party.
- I plan to have the book edited by this date to be published on time.
- I plan to write x amount of chapters per day.
- I plan to write the outline.
- I plan on having a great idea for a book.

Be S.M.A.R.T. With Your Goal Setting

Specific – Be precise and concise about what you want to achieve.
Measurable – Create checkpoints to measure your progress.
Attainable – No pie in the sky ambitions, use realistic grounded goals.
Relevant – Make sure the goal has purpose.
Timely – A realistic timeline for completion.

EXAMPLE

S – I plan to write a book about entrepreneurship rules by x date.
M – Each day I have written x amount of words and chapters.
A – Once written, I plan on selling 5,000 copies & digital downloads.
R – The purpose is to spread knowledge.
T – This book should be completed within 1 month.

Break Large Tasks Into Smaller Ones

It helps combat procrastination if you aren't overwhelmed by the major task, but see it simply as a series of smaller tasks that can be accomplished much easier.

EXAMPLE – Write the book > How many chapters > How many sub points > Write paragraphs on each sub point

Keep A Visual Of Your Goals

If your goals are out of sight, they are out of mind. Make sure you place your goals somewhere you see them daily.

Mark Goals Off As You Go

It is extremely satisfying to be able to cross off items on the list. It will help keep you moving forward when you see how far you have come.

Record Everything

Keep notes, research, follow ups and use this as the living version of your goals. Plus it helps to have more materials you can use for future editions or behind the scenes footage.

Don't Stop Until The Mission Is Complete

Change your dates if necessary, but most importantly you must keep going. You've got this!

Time Management

Now that you've got your plan completed, let's discuss the best way to use your time effectively to get it done. Understand, time is a finite resource. What is spent, you will not get back. Use it wisely.

- *Get A Planner*

In order to maximize your time, you must document how that time is spent. There are some great calendar apps such as Google Calendar, Any.do,or Microsoft's Outlook. While others prefer something more tangible such as a physical planner. Amazingly, when you write things down, you are more inclined to do them.

- *Time Blocking*

In addition to having a planner with the days, find one that has the time slots as well. I utilized this technique from my days at Cutco. When you have your day mapped out, you don't have to be stressed about not having enough time to knock out your tasks. With a specific time block to handle something, you are less likely to procrastinate because you know that you have only so much time to accomplish the task. And you become more efficient in how you handle your day. This includes scheduling time for lunch, leisure activities (including family and down time and breaks.

- *Take Time To Set Your Week*

I prefer using Sunday as the day to set up the rest of my week. That way when you get up on Monday, you are ready to go. The important thing is to pick a day, map out the week and add/subtract as you go.

- *Schedule For Issues*

Build time in your block for potential issues such as traveling or possible meeting over runs so your next task can start on time. If you are 5 minutes late in the early part of your day, it can quickly end up being an hour by lunch.

- *Take Time To Disconnect*

Unplug from social media and your devices so that you can reset and get grounded with yourself. Find time to meditate and center yourself. Too often we get caught up in the motion of our day and forget to take time to be still. It's ok, you have the time to do so if you plan it correctly and the outside world will be there when you get back.

EXAMPLE OF THE RULE

Montero Hill grew up poor in Atlanta yet knew he was destined for greatness. But how? With no resources and feeling alone, he sat on his couch scouring the internet for memes and followed a popular Nicki Minaj fan account. Summer 2018, he dropped out of college and posted various songs to Soundcloud with little success. That Halloween, newly dubbed Lil Nas X discovered a beat on YouTube from a Dutch producer named YoungKio. He bought the track for only $30 from a music licensing website named BeatStars. Inspired by the part-trap, part-country beat, Lil Nas X created "Old Town Road."

Released in December 2018, he featured the song over scenes from the popular Western themed video game, "Red Dead Redemption 2." He made the song intentionally short to be quotable, catchy and force the listener to want play it again. By the following March, the meme went viral as users made their own version of the tune and posted it on TikTok via the #yeehawchallenge. Users went from normal then in a split second turn into a country cowboy or girl complete with lassos, plaid shirts and Stetsons.

Columbia Records signed him a week after the song debuted on the charts. Then they put Billy Ray Cyrus on the remix and by summer, it was the #1 song in the country complete with its own controversy due to the Billboard country charts removing it from their lists. By 1st quarter 2020, he went on to earn 2 Grammy's, the movie "Rambo: Last Blood" used the song for its promo campaign and he even had a Super Bowl commercial with Doritos. In one year, he went from sitting on the couch as a college drop out to mega star because he had a plan and executed it perfectly!

> "Spectacular
> achievement is
> always preceded
> by unspectacular
> preparation."
>
> – ROBERT H. SCHULLER

Jah concludes, "in business, you have to sit and make a plan of action in order for the plan to survive. That's how you feed your family, plus you have other people around you and that's how they feed theirs. In any business, any business owner that says they make 100% of their money has not planned it out correctly. You have expenses and obligations. Unforeseen circumstances that you have to pay. If you don't pay yourself, your business will fail. You will be depending on your employees to pay the business. What happens when they fall off? Your business will fail. You have to pay yourself."

WARNING

Don't get so caught up planning that you forget the action. All the planning in the world won't get the work done. You must execute your plan. Don't be upset about the results you didn't get from the work you didn't do.

YOUR MISSION

Your mission is to think about what you want to do and use the techniques in this chapter to write an effective plan and timeline to get it done. Then work your plan.

Thrill Da Playa advises you to "follow your calling. You get your instruction as a musician and vibe from a higher power. Stay in touch with that higher power, and don't wish to integrate with a lower power to try and power up. That's not how you survive for the long haul. You have to follow your plan and listen to that voice and implement when you can. Every release or project may not bring you big numbers but do everything with quality and care."

PLAN ACCORDINGLY

* * *

NOTES TO SELF // TODAY I LEARNED ... // MY NEXT STEP IS ...

6

STOP PROCRASTINATING — GET 'ER DONE!!!

"Procrastination is like masturbation, it feels good in the moment, but in the end you only f*ck yourself."
TYLER TARR (*Team Leader, Cutco*)

===

"Do not be upset by the results you didn't get from the work you didn't do."
CARL WILLIS (*Broadcaster, WJLA-TV, Washington, DC*)

===

"I fly with the stars in the skies / I am no longer trying to survive
I believe that life is a prize / But to live doesn't mean you're alive"
NICKI MINAJ - *"Moment 4 Life"*

===

"[Cuz] One day you're here and the next day you're gone"
BUN B - *"One Day"*

===

"You've got to realize that the world's a test / You can only do your best and let Him do the rest
You've got your life, you've got your health / So quit procrastinating and push it yourself"
CEE-LO GREEN - *"In Due Time"*

===

"Tomorrow may never come / Life is not promised
Tomorrow may never show up / This life is not promised"
MOS DEF - *"Umi Says"*

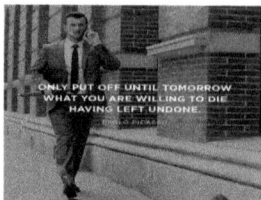

Full disclosure, my biggest daily demon is procrastination. The lazy thought of 'there is plenty of time so I will get it done later' has become a productivity killer. It is commonly paired with other misguided mental notes such as, 'I work better under pressure.' I used to be very good at procrastinating just enough to get the job done and achieve positive results. The problem is that when you put yourself under that kind of stress, mistakes get made, the ability to pivot if there is a problem is greatly reduced and the quality of the work suffers. Especially if you have other people waiting on you to complete the project. You quickly learn that an emergency on your part does not necessitate one on theirs.

I had to learn that it is much easier and better for my spirit if I do a little bit at a time and work towards the larger goal. Otherwise, you are walking a tightrope without a net and anything can happen if you have just one wrong slip. Perhaps you have a procrastination problem as well. Because even the greats like Bigga Rankin admit, "when I was growing up, I was a big procrastinator. But, you must be accountable."

Think of it this way, spoiler alert, we are all going to die. That means that everyday we have here on Earth is a blessing and a chance for you to live the way that you want to live. If you are not living the way you want, that means you should be working everyday to accomplish this. Wouldn't you rather have more days living your dream than wishing you could? Does pushing off what you need to finish feel better than you living the life you want?

Each day you have three measurements as to what kind of day it was - a positive day, a negative day or a zero day.

A positive day is one where you put honest effort towards your goal. Even if it is 10 minutes, 1 hour or the full day, all positive energy builds momentum towards your main mission.

A negative day is when it seems to come from hell and sets you back. These are bound to happen when you play The Game. But, if you shake it off, get back up and keep moving forward, you can bounce back by pushing through towards your goal. Then you turn it around or make the next day a positive day. Aim to have more positive days than negative days during a week.

However, the one type of day you should never have if you want to win The Game, is a zero day. A zero day is when you do nothing towards your goal. Everyday you must do at least one activity towards your goal. Don't get me wrong, it is good to have an occasional day off to reset. Just understand that for every zero day there is one less day you have to live in your glory. So, get to it now. Everyday! Consistency is the key to victory. The more you work towards your goal, the faster it will come to you.

Even if you only have one hour to spare. Imagine using that one hour every day. Over the course of a year, that is 365 hours that you can put towards whatever idea or project you have. Think of what you can accomplish in that time frame! Remember, there are no time machines to help you get back time that is wasted. And all of the little actions add up to big things.

"You still be wasting days away, nah had I never saved a day"
T.I. - *"Live Your Life"*

Tupac Shakur once dropped the line, "when I die, I wanna be a living legend / affiliated with this muthaf*ckin' Game." So, when he died at 25 years old, he did just that because of his work ethic. In only 5 years (including one he spent in jail), he dropped 4 classic albums (12 million sold) then 7 more *AFTER* he died, including several double albums that sold over 13 million units combined. Not to mention the 7 movies he starred in plus a memorable TV episode of "A Different World." He never wasted a day and maximized each recording session often working on multiple songs at the same time. Imagine if he decided to procrastinate. Would he have been able to be immortalized the way he has been without all of that material? If you want to be great, don't waste your time.

As the promo expert, Kingpin succinctly states, now is the time to "get off the couch, network and invest in yourself." Science says it takes as little as 21 consistent days for a habit to form, but the average is pegged at 66. By the time you reach 90, your new methodology should be stuck. However, it's up to you to keep it going. If you relapse, do not stress over it, just begin again. There are great daily tracker apps such as LoseIt! for weight loss, Habitica if you want to make tracking a fun video game challenge or Strides if you want a clean and simple chain tracker.

For all of my physics fans, Newton (the guy that discovered gravity when the apple hit him in the head) has 3 laws of motion that apply perfectly to your mission.

- *Newton's 1st Law* – An object will remain at rest until acted on by an outside force
- *Newton's 2nd Law* – Force = Mass x Acceleration
- *Newton's 3rd Law* – For every action, there is an equal and opposite reaction

Plus, physics has an actual formula for getting work done. It is $W = F * D$ which means work equals force times direction. Essentially all of this means that until you act upon your desires to get the ball rolling, nothing will ever happen and you can't be mad that you are unfulfilled. But, once you get your mighty momentum going, you will be unstoppable. So, get moving! You can do it!

TOOLS TO FIGHT PROCRASTINATION

1. Break large tasks into smaller tasks. If one sees the mountain, mentally one is quick to tap out because the task seems so insurmountable. Even if it is only a molehill. Kristin Dungee calls this "compartmentalization [which is] to focus on the task at hand, not the 4-5 you have to do."

2. Do the one thing. Once you get started on that one thing, the momentum will carry you through to the next thing.

3. Set realistic deadlines and hold yourself accountable. Even better, have someone help you be accountable if necessary. A good accountability buddy is harder to con and will keep you on track.

4. Getting it done is better than waiting for it to be perfect. Perfection is often a procrastination co-conspirator. We often don't want to do it or turn it in unless it is perfect. Then we get so caught up and put the pressure on us when it is not done perfectly that we don't do it at all.

5. It is better to overdo it than to overthink it. Get out of your head, count to 3 and get it started. Just like when you are hesitant to jump in the pool because it is cold, when you do a full body splash, after the initial shock your surroundings feel great as you navigate the waters.

6. Forgive yourself for earlier procrastination transgressions. Recognize that you are where you are, it is what it is and then get it going! You double down on wasted time when you dwell on it.

7. Remove distractions including your phone and stay offline. Once you get distracted, then the process resets itself and it will lead to further procrastination.

8. Find your groove. For some, music will help create a good space, some prefer silence. Whatever it is, find it quickly and get to work.

9. Set a clock. Work your time (start with one hour) and after your buzzer goes off. Take a short break. Then get back to work. It helps to build momentum and confidence that you are getting things done without a burnout.

10. Reward yourself. Treat yourself to something nice once you get that task completed. You deserve it!

APPS TO HELP YOU FIGHT PROCRASTINATION

1. *Todoist* – This creates a prioritized list of tasks that need to be knocked out
2. *Focusmate* - Helps you find an accountability buddy
3. *Stickk* - Forces you to handle your biz or you pay the financial cost for flaking out
4. *Brain.fm* - Uses music to keep you in the proper zone
5. *Toggle* - Logs your productivity time
6. *Offtime* - Takes away the distractions on your phone

YOUR ASSIGNMENT

Get a planner and keep track of your days. Mark what kind of day you had. Was it a + / - or 0. Be truthful, you are only hurting or helping yourself. Look at it once a week to track your progress. Then, stay consistent. After that first week, then a month, then 3 months, then a year and see where you stand with your goals. I bet you will be satisfied with the results.

NOTES TO SELF // TODAY I LEARNED ... // MY NEXT STEP IS ...

7

PUT SOME RESPECT ON MY NAME

"I don't know what you do for your respect, but I'mma die for mine!"
T.I. - *"ASAP"*

===

"The only thing I got in this world is my balls and my word, and I don't break 'em for nobody!"
TONY MONTANA - *"Scarface"*

* * *

Respect is defined as a feeling of deep admiration for someone or something elicited by their abilities, qualities or achievements. In addition, it is a due regard for the feelings, wishes, rights or traditions of others. Simply put, respect is *THE* main currency in The Game. It has more gravitas than money or power. With respect, you won't need money and power will be bestowed upon you. Doors will open and opportunities will present themselves. Without it, you will not be able to achieve the goals you have set forth. Respect is even more important than money and it is the cornerstone of any power base. There have been plenty of times in my career where respect gets a meeting or access where money would not be as effective. Money is only as good as long as you have it in life, whereas respect can last longer than a lifetime.

Respect can be difficult to earn and easy to lose. Once it is lost, it is incredibly hard to regain. That is why in The Game, the currency of respect is prized above all else. There are plenty of gravestones and prison numbers filled because of an action that was perceived as a lack respect. My mother's greatest lesson to me was to "never let someone disrespect you." If someone disrespects you in the slightest, it is a sliding scale where it may start small, but eventually it will become a cascading effect that will overwhelm you. And you will never recover.

For example, in the movie "Life," Claude was asked to give up his cornbread. Claude's friend, Ray taught him that in the prison culture, if you give up your cornbread one time, you will be giving up other things for the duration of your stay - a blatant form of disrespect. The Rule is that it is important to always fight and protect your cornbread (aka your respect from all those that wish to take it from you. Therefore, disrespect must be handled accordingly if you are to rise in the ranks and win The Game.

The messed up thing is that the balance between respect and disrespect is so thin and precarious. One misstep can blow up a deal or the right steps can be very lucrative. You must be very cautious of how to show and prove your respect. There have been nights at The Venue where lack of respect creates a problem and other times when a show of respect solves a problem.

The American Meme, OG Magnum has this to say about respect, "every amazing experience I have had in my travels around the globe have been based on respect. That's what it is totally about. Hold your own values, but respect everyone around you." And as far as disrespect, he continues, "people mistake pride for respect and get volatile over pride issues. Once you are so secure in yourself, no one will be able to bother you again."

HOW DO I GAIN RESPECT?

First, you must understand that respect is a two-way street. It is not given, it must be mutually earned and it will take time. This is done in a variety of ways such as shared experiences, commonalities, understanding of one's struggle, status / position, mutual acquaintances, and how you treat someone can all lead to added respect levels. But, the most important way to gain respect is to do what you say. If you honor your word and follow through on what you say, then that is the strongest bond you can make.

OG Magnum notes that first you must have, "respect for yourself and respect for other people. You must follow protocols and engage in polite behavior. I have definitely inadvertently broken protocols because I don't pay attention or I am misguided by other people and I didn't know how The Game is played."

DJ Lil Boy explains the art of respect further, "you always have to remember where you at. The rules in your hood may not necessarily be the same as where you are at. You can't go to a Muslim country talking about, 'where's the pork at?' Ask the locals, especially taxi drivers, bell hops, and maids. They will tell you who the man is in the area and what the Rules are in that area that you must abide by. Plus, they can help get you whatever you may need."

Respect can also be gained through fear and love. Although they are on opposite ends of the same spectrum, the same Rules can be applied. Both emotions are very strong. The author of "The Prince," Niccolo Machiavelli teaches it is better to be feared than loved when you cannot be both. But, if you only adopt one extreme, eventually you will lose respect and be toppled. For instance, if you only earn respect through fear like the Empire in "Star Wars," one mistake and your enemies will swarm to take you down at the first crack of weakness. You will always be on the lookout for enemies and slight transgressions. Your paranoia will be extreme and you will constantly be stressed and on edge. Therefore, it is not sustainable in the long run.

If you earn respect only though love, eventually your resolve will be tested to see if you are weak. Then you must demonstrate a well timed execution of power to show that you are not to be trifled with.

You must find a proper balance to properly navigate The Game. Respect is mandatory for you to achieve your goals. Get it whenever and however possible and never let it go.

This is how DJ Princess Cut gained her respect. "I always had a deep love with music. I didn't have the slightest clue on how to make it, but I spent a lot of time within the culture like at music stores. I met with DJs throughout the city and through the power of networking I was always in the stores seeking information from them along with practicing and I started getting recommendation for gigs. It's important for you to surround yourself in it, embrace it and submerge yourself in it and 9 times out of 10, you will get great results in it. If not 10 times out of 10. Along with studying and practicing, I looked up DJ battles online and became fascinated with it, being able to look and see what they were doing really helped me."

She continues, "I got my first tour through the power of networking 1.5 - 3 years into my craft. The Outlawz were in need of a DJ for a tour. The follow up, once you have the opportunity, you must maintain it and show and prove. Leave no room for doubt. You never know when the opportunity will come. That was my first tour. It took me to Australia, Ireland, Saudi Arabia and I knew this was for me."

She concludes, "once you show and prove, you will gain respect. I've had older DJs try to cut into my time and I've had to speak up for myself. 'No, this is my time!' Don't hold it in if you have an issue, speak on it right then. Especially as a woman, handle it on sight."

RESPECT ACTIONS

Strong Handshake – The handshake is a valuable first impression tool. It can determine how much of a backbone you have, how cool you can be and set the tone of the conversation. Be forewarned, a limp handshake will have you labeled as weak before you even speak.

Eye Contact – You can read your opponent by the look in their eye. It is true, the eyes are the window to the soul.

Proper Gifts / Presents – Make sure you understand who you are giving these to and what the gift represents. If you present it incorrectly, you will inadvertently fall in the disrespect category.

Saying Yes / No Sir or Ma'am - This is even more true in the South. If you don't address your elders or veteran Game players with these pleasantries, your target may feel slighted.

Manners – Having proper manners at lunch or a meeting go a long way.

Being Punctual – Showing respect to people's time is a great way to ingratiate yourself. If you are to be late, call ahead and bring something more than an apology (coffee, donuts, bagels, etc). Going back to what I learned during my Alpha days, showing up on time is late and early is on time.

Reciprocity – Doing for them as you would like for them to do for you.

Returning A Lighter - On the surface, this may seem trivial but returning a lighter demonstrates character, honor, and trust. A lighter is a big deal to a smoker and they are accustomed to people constantly taking their lighter. If you are the one that returns it, it shows them that they can trust you and you will earn their respect.

Asking For Advice – Most people like to talk about themselves. If you ask them a question that preys upon their experiences, they will appreciate you for wanting to learn and you might pick up some wonderful nuggets along the way. Either way, you will have earned their respect.

Attire - People will gain or lose respect for you based on your attire. Your mission when you leave the house should always be to be sharp, to be crisp and to be clean. Fair or unfair, people judge on appearances. If you are sloppy or well put together, people will address you accordingly.

Accepting Responsibility - If something went wrong and it was on you, accept it, fix it and move forward. This is a great way to gain respect in the face of a possible conflict. Displacing blame or not working to find a solution loses face and you will not be looked at kindly.

Standing Up For Yourself - This technique is important because if you do not stand up for yourself and "go off" at least once, people will think you have no backbone and deliberately say and do things to disrespect you. Once you stand up for yourself, usually they back off and go after someone weaker. Be mindful about how often you do it and how you do it, otherwise you could play yourself out of position like Dame Dash, former CEO of Roc-A-Fella Records.

Julia Beverly adds, "the music business can be cut throat. You can't let people walk over you and take advantage. Be firm in what you want, play The Game like everyone else is playing The Game. If you are a pushover or scared to step up and take control of things, you will be taken advantage of. If it means as a woman you get called a bitch, stand your ground if that's what needs to happen for you to achieve your goals, who cares what they say about you?"

RESPECTING YOUR ENEMIES

In The Game, if you are to be successful, eventually you will have rivals or enemies. If you ain't got haters, you ain't doing it right. However, you should always show them the proper respect even as you plan to annihilate them. This serves two purposes. First, it's like fattening up the pig before the kill. Your enemy may take a misstep or not press fully due to your show of respect. In fact, it may blindside them to your eventual strike. Second, you should never underestimate your enemy. It helps you keep your edge against them.

NBA greats Horace Grant and Scottie Pippen have many anecdotes about how before a game Michael Jordan would be smiling and joking with an opponent before the game. Why? When Jordan got his opponent to relax, even momentarily, it allowed him to strike first and gain an advantage.

HOW CAN I LOSE RESPECT?

Respect can be lost easily by, among other things, not adhering to the Rules of the situation, showing up late, doing something to injure another party (physically, emotionally, financially, etc), saying something that is out of pocket (demeaning or out of place), siding against them in a conflict, looking down on someone or not holding up your end of the agreed upon bargain. But, the most egregious of all is not abiding by your word.

OG Magnum warns, "this [Game] is rough and people are always trying to finesse things out of you. You have to have agreements in writing. And even then, they will sometimes try to pay you a fraction of what is owed. I have to hold my ground and be a d!ck in order to get what is agreed upon." Afterwards, a new respect is forged and the likelihood of that happening again has diminished. At least until the next janky promoter tries it. So, you have to always be on guard.

Once again, understand that loss of respect will only lead to bigger problems and impede you on your goals of being successful. Usually a loss of respect is accompanied by some form of punishment for breaking the rules. It might come physically, loss of opportunities, loss of access or some another way, but rest assured, there will be consequences. The only way back is to apologize to the aggrieved party and offer some form of tribute. Then never make that mistake again and if possible, work to rebuild that trust over time.

Regarding disrespect, DJ Lil Boy shares this, "if you disrespect on the road there are one of two ways you can handle it. In London one time with T-Pain, we had to fight our way out and get home by any means necessary. Or, the other route is humble. In Inglewood in LA, one time I was in a Blood neighborhood and I said, 'what up, cuz!' The first thing they did was ask where I was from, and when I said 'Florida,' they gave me a pass because I didn't know that 'cuz' was a Crip word. When I played it humble, they checked me without it going crazy."

* * *

NOTES TO SELF // TODAY I LEARNED ... // MY NEXT STEP IS ...

8

COMMUNICATION IS KEY

"What we've got here is failure to communicate."
CAPTAIN, *"Cool Hand Luke"*

===

"I've learned that people will forget what you said, people will forget what you did, but people will never forget how you made them feel."
MAYA ANGELOU (*Poet Laureate*

===

"It is better to keep one's mouth shut and be thought a fool, than to open it and resolve all doubt."
ABRAHAM LINCOLN, (*16th President of the United States of America*

===

"Once a word leaves your mouth, you cannot chase it back even with the swiftest horse."
CHINESE PROVERB

* * *

In The Game, proper communication is a two-way street. The key is to make sure we are headed in the same direction as those we communicate with so they can flow with you. That is the biggest take away I learned from my Communication Degree at Florida State. It sounds a lot easier than it is at times, but proper communication is a skill that you must master in order to be successful. This is how you develop what is known as your "Talk Game."

Your Talk Game is the ability to communicate effectively in order to cajole, persuade and help others follow along with your point of view to achieve a goal that benefits you. All successful players of The Game pride themselves on their Talk Game.

In addition, you must master a strong BS detector. This is the ability to hear or feel what someone is trying to communicate with you, but your vibes pick up an undercurrent of falsehoods or misinformation. You have to develop this skill or you will fall prey to whatever someone tells you and be subjected to avoidable setbacks.

In this chapter, we will go over tips, hurdles and ways to become a better communicator. Without it, your messages will be miscommunicated and not be received well enough for you to accomplish your goals.

The most important Rule in communication is to always remember that words have power. Be very mindful that no one can read your mind so it is *extremely* important that as you translate what you are thinking into words and actions, you must understand that once your message is sent out into the world, it cannot be taken back. So, make sure that whatever messages you transmit are exactly as you intend. Otherwise, you will spend valuable time and energy backtracking as you play damage control.

TYPES OF COMMUNICATION

There are four main types of communication verbal, non-verbal, written and visual. But, what they all have in common is that there will always be a sender and a receiver. We will go over each of them to help you get acquainted.

VERBAL – This mode of communication uses words to get your message across. This is the usual method most of us use on a daily basis, usually combined with one of the other forms. These include phone conversations, face-to-face chats, speeches, etc. This form of communication also has 4 subsets:

1. *Intrapersonal* – This is the inner dialogue you have with yourself.

2. *Interpersonal* – This is a conversation you have one-on-one with someone.

3. *Small Group* – This is used with two or more people usually in a boardroom, classroom, or team meeting space. Since you will be dealing with more than one person, if this is not carefully controlled, it can develop into chaos.

4. *Public* – This is usually for large group settings like when giving a speech to a filled auditorium.

NON-VERBAL – This form of communication relies on processing thoughts and feelings without using words or sounds such as gestures, body language, facial expressions, eye contact, clothing, tone, or other cues to convey a point. Use this in combination with other modes of communication to accentuate your message.

WRITTEN – This medium is conveyed through written words. These include letters, text, journals, emails, reports, articles, memos, etc. The best thing about this form of communication is that before it is sent, you have a chance to go over it as many times as necessary to make sure it is correct. In addition, the recipient will read the communication with their own frame of mind as a reference. Meaning, if they are upset, they will find an undercurrent of negativity with your message. Be judicious in what and how you send these messages, because sometimes it is better said than written.

VISUAL – This is when one uses pictures as a way to get their point across. Examples include emojis, photography, visual aids, symbols, signs, designs, etc.

Have you ever heard the phrase, it's not what you say, but how you say it? Well, Dr. Albert Mehrabian, a communication expert, coined the "7-38-55 Rule" which states that when a message is put forth, the recipient measures the message with words at 7%, tone of voice at 38% and body language accounting for 55%. This means that 93% of the messages you put out are received non-verbally. How does this translate? People will pay more attention to how you deliver a message than the message itself.

With this in mind, here are a few of the non-verbal cues that trigger the hijacking of your verbal message and some proper techniques to have your messages received the way it is intended.

1. *VOCAL TONE* – Your speaking style, pitch, rate of speed and volume all add up to how your message is received. If you just had an argument with your significant other and they told you "it's fine" but with a cold undertone, you know that things are not as fine as they said. Tone matters.

2. *FIDGETING* – If you can't sit still or always checking your phone, the receiver is noticing your movements and not your message. It conveys nervousness, boredom or disinterest. None of which are good for you to be heard correctly.

3. *FACIAL EXPRESSIONS* – Your face and eyes will tell the truth when your words don't. If you are at odds internally with the outgoing message, be mindful that your face doesn't snitch on you.

4. *HEAD MOVEMENTS* – If you are in a meeting and you are getting head nods in agreement, then you know you are on the right track. But, if you are getting head shakes, then you know you need to change your message or open the floor to questions to get them back on your side. Pay attention to your audience, they will tell you what they are thinking if you know what to listen for.

5. *HAND GESTURES* – Speaking with your hands can be threatening for some, especially if the conversation tends to get passionate. Also, if your hands are shaking then the recipient will pick up on that and know you are nervous which may undercut your message. Be mindful and when in doubt, put your hands in your pocket, on the table, or behind your back.

6. *BODY POSTURE* – Your body language will tell the receiver everything. If you are slouched, you are bored or uninterested. If you are leaning forward, you are engaged. If you are standing tall, you are confident. Your posture matters, act accordingly.

7. *PHYSICAL DISTANCE* – Everyone has a circle of personal space, in America, it is usually about 18". When it is invaded, your message may be affected or if there is too much space, your message may be ignored. Touching can be precarious, so be careful with it. Even if you mean no harm, not everyone appreciates a slap on the back or an unsolicited arm touch. In the era of the #MeToo Movement, an uninvited touch can go in the wrong direction very quickly. Be careful.

If a potential client recognizes or picks up on these non-verbal cues and receives a negative message, you may lose out on a deal even if you are saying all of the right things. Conversely, if you use these techniques to your advantage and learn to read between the lines, you can use the unspoken information to create opportunities for yourself.

* * *

In order to communicate effectively, you must want to. This is a process that only gets easier with identification and practice. Below are The 7 C's of Effective Communication and a few tips on how to implement them. With these under your belt, your messages will be well received.

THE 7 C'S OF EFFECTIVE COMMUNICATION

1. *CLARITY* – Be clear with your message. Use the K.I.S.S. Method, Keep It Simple Stupid.

2. *CONCISE* – Use as few words as possible to save time and reduce the chance of using the wrong ones.

3. *CORRECT* – Use accurate facts and figures, proper use of grammar, spelling and language. If the receiver is picking apart your message due to errors, then the message will be lost.

4. *COMPLETE* – You must convey all the facts required by the receiver to comprehend the message. Giving partial information leads to confusion.

5. *CONSIDERATION* – Understand who your audience is and speak to them accordingly. If you use big words to a simple crowd, your message will not come across the way you want.

6. *COURTESY* – Use your personality to connect to the feelings of your communication target. If you don't connect with them, then they won't care to hear what you have to say.

7. *CONCRETE* – Your message must be clear with nothing left to the imagination. Interpretation will lead to your message being watered down and muddled.

Bonus C - *CONFRONTATION* - Most people are afraid of confrontation because it is uncomfortable and often unpleasant. But, in the world of communication, confrontation can be a good thing. There can often be pent up walls built with things that aren't said. Constructive confrontation can pierce those walls and get everything out in the open to be discussed. Clearing the air can help with future dialog and relations. This is especially true if you find yourself in a 'he said' vs 'she said' situation. Get both sides to the table and have a direct conversation to get to the crux of the conflict. Never be afraid of the difficult conversation, it only leads to growth.

TIPS TO BECOME A BETTER COMMUNICATOR

1. *TAKE TIME* – Take a moment to understand your purpose of the message, who will be receiving it and what is your end game. Why and who you are communicating with in the first place will get you to understand the point you are trying to get across.

2. *SET THE RIGHT TONE* – As the sender, you select the method, mood, message and delivery. Make sure you set one of willingness to listen and an openness to learn.

3. *BE CLEAR & CONCISE* – As the efficient accountant from TV's hit show, "The Office," Kevin would say, "why use more word, when few do trick?"

4. *BE AN ACTIVE LISTENER* – Everyone wants to be heard, not dictated to. Give the receiver the chance to know you care about what they have to say too. Use head nods, insert an occasional, "I understand" or "what I'm hearing is…" and be genuine.

5. *ASK FOR & ALLOW FEEDBACK* – As long as the feedback is constructive, listen to what your receiver says, it will help you in the long run.

6. *BE PRESENT* – Often, we are more worried about what we are going to say next than what your communication partner is presenting and we may miss vital messages. Take your time and be in the moment. A good conversation is like a tennis match with the messages going back and forth.

7. *DO NOT DOMINATE* – Give your recipient a chance to speak. If you dominate the conversation, your message will be rejected. Don't go more than three sentences without hearing a response. If you want to be heard, try learning to listen as well.

8. *DON'T DICTATE THOUGHTS & FEELINGS* – Never tell someone how they feel or think. They already know. It is up to you to hear what and why they feel that way. Offer empathy and acceptance of their message, it will go a long way for you to be heard as well.

9. *BODY LANGUAGE* – Use head nods, eye contact, lean forward, and engage in what they are saying.

10. *COMMUNICATE THEIR WAY* – Understand who your audience is and reach out to them using the way they communicate best.

11. *CONTROL YOUR EMOTIONS* – If the conversation is a charged one, make sure you keep your cool. The second emotions go unchecked, effective communication is over. Then it turns into an argument where each side fights to be right, not to be heard. Never send outgoing messages in anger. This includes texts, emails and calls. Once it goes out, sometimes an apology won't be enough to repair the damage.

12. *SAY IT WITH A SMILE* - Since most communication is non-verbal, it is important to give off a positive vibe. Nothing does that more than saying

your message with a smile. It helps put people at ease and therefore, more receptive to your message. Even over the phone, you can hear when someone is smiling.

WARNING - BARRIERS TO EFFECTIVE COMMUNICATION

Psychological Barriers - The psychological state of the receiver will influence how the message is received. For example, if someone has personal worries and is stressed, they may be preoccupied by personal concerns and not be as receptive to the message. Stress management is an important personal skill that affects our interpersonal relationships. Anger is another example of a psychological barrier to communication. When we are angry it is easy to say things that we may later regret and also to misinterpret what others are saying. More generally, people with low self-esteem may be less assertive and therefore may not feel comfortable communicating. They may feel shy about saying how they really feel, or read negative sub-texts into messages they hear.

Physiological Barriers - Physiological barriers may result from the receiver's physical state. For example, a receiver with reduced hearing may not grasp the entirety of a spoken conversation, especially if there is significant background noise.

Physical Barriers - An example of a physical barrier to communication is geographic distance between the sender and receiver(s). Communication is generally easier over shorter distances as more communication channels are available and less technology is required. Although modern technology often serves to reduce the impact of physical barriers, the advantages and disadvantages of each communication channel should be understood so that an appropriate channel can be used to overcome the physical barriers.

Attitudinal Barriers - Attitudinal barriers are behaviors or perceptions that prevent people from communicating effectively. Attitudinal barriers to communication may result from personality conflicts, poor management, resistance to change, or a lack of motivation. Effective receivers of messages should attempt to overcome their own attitudinal barriers to facilitate effective communication.

* * *

NOTES TO SELF // TODAY I LEARNED ... // MY NEXT STEP IS ...

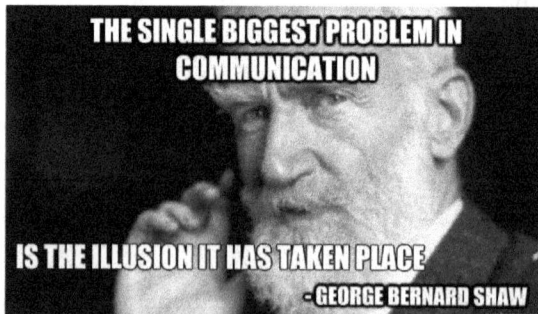

THE SINGLE BIGGEST PROBLEM IN COMMUNICATION

IS THE ILLUSION IT HAS TAKEN PLACE
- GEORGE BERNARD SHAW

9

I GOT THE HOOK UP —
RELATIONSHIPS

"Relationships are the key to this business."
TJ CHAPMAN

* * *

Simply put, relationships are the lifeblood of The Game. Some may feel they can be successful on their own. The truth is, nothing can be accomplished without help from others - hence, the need for relationships. Want to get a record played? You will need a relationship with the DJ or program director. Want to get your artist signed? You will need a relationship with an A&R. Want to throw a party? You need a relationship with the venue owner/manager. Without proper relationships, you will exponentially increase the difficulty of your Game.

TJ Chapman puts it succinctly, "I'm all about relationships. My whole business, life and brand is based on relationships with people. Those relationships are what allows me to make moves and accomplish things that someone else can't."

Your goal should be to have a someone for everything and every situation. Need a caterer for a party, I've got someone for that. Need help getting your story out? I've got a media plug for that. Want to get the city involved or off your back? I've got a city councilman for that. Need a photo shoot? I've got a photographer for that. The more people you know or more essentially, the more who know you, the better your Game will be played.

The idea is that whatever your need is, you should have a representative for that. If you don't have one, get one. Even if it is someone at the bottom of the totem pole, at least they are an 'in' to the facility that allows you to work your way up the ladder. Remember, even the person answering calls at a central desk knows who you need to talk to, when they are available and most importantly, allow you to be connected. That is, if they like you.

So what if you have money and can buy whatever you need? True indeed, money can get you in the door and perhaps take care of a few things for you. In fact, you should make sure you pay people accordingly for their time and efforts. But, if you just pay people without attempting to build a relationship what will actually happen is first, you will over pay for your needs because people will see you as a mark or quick way to get a check. Secondly, as soon as the money runs out, since you didn't take time to build a proper relationship, that person will disappear and will be very difficult to reach until you find another check for them.

TJ Chapman explains, "Money is a double edge sword. It's beautiful having budgets and money because being in business and being an entrepreneur, period, can be expensive. And who knows when you will get money and you still have expenses so you have to know how to juggle everything else. A lot of people with money feel like money takes precedence over the importance of the relationship and they base everything on the money. Depending on how you approach it, especially in this Game, it can be a gift and a curse. Yeah, you can buy whatever you need. But by doing that, you are also being looked at and being labeled as a target. They see you have money and spending money, they want to get some of that money."

He continues, "you pigeon hole yourself and you can never get out of it because you've been labeled with money. It's cool to have money, but money doesn't exceed the importance of the relationships because with the right relationships, I don't need no money."

A relationship built on mutual respect is much stronger than a relationship bought.

For example, when Khao (producer, T.I. "Why You Wanna") decided he wanted to be a solo artist, his tag line was "the only artist that pays." And that's what he did. He paid DJs to play his music, he paid record pools to service his project, he paid top dollar to consultants to promote it. When the money was flowing, his song was everywhere, but as soon as the money dried up, you didn't hear of him or his song again.

Bigga Rankin concludes with, "relationships are way bigger than money, but you have to have money to pay bills. I've done more free stuff than I charge for. Later in my life, free is too expensive. Sometimes when you give them an inch, they want a yard. They just want more and more. You can't help everyone."

RESPECT YOUR RELATIONSHIPS

By now you have heard the expression; you never get a second chance to make a first impression. This is extremely important in relationship building. The first time someone meets you, they will determine if they like you, want to do business with you or never want to see you again in life. So, how do you tilt the odds in your favor?

You will meet a new contact one of two ways, by random encounter (this includes social media, in an elevator, at a social gathering, etc.) or by introduction (via a mutual associate). The main difference is if you mess up a contact that you met through a random encounter, you just may never be able to catch that person again for any interaction. You will be burned and never be able to utilize that contact for any future business and depending on who they know, they may spread negative word about you which will damage your reputation. And negative word travels much faster than positive word.

However, a new contact via introduction by a mutual associate bears additional weight. This means that if you mess this up, then the mutual associate is put in a situation of either cutting you loose or risk damaging their prior relationship. Which means you potentially could lose multiple connections. Because more times than not, they will do self-preservation damage control and reduce their exposure to your mistakes.

The reasoning is, you were introduced on the face of your associate. They vouched for you being a good business person, so they could be punished for your mistakes. Think of the movie, "Donnie Brasco." Lefty had to answer for Brasco being an FBI informant because Lefty introduced him to his colleagues. Similarly, if you mess it up, your reputation and the relationship will be sleeping with the fishes.

The lesson is no matter how you are introduced; take new potential relationships seriously. Your business life depends on them.

This is a lesson DJ Demp takes seriously. "My relationships been cool for years and [for Demp Week] I don't book them, they come pull up. Most artists stay for 2-3 days for my event because they f*ck with me."

Additionally, once you've made it in The Game and now you are the one people clamor to get the attention of, do not be callous and step on the ones coming up. These are the people of the next generation. Be kind and grant them even a few minutes of your time. Odds are they look up to you so treat them right and you can build a loyal legion of soldiers.

You will find that as you move up, it becomes more difficult to keep your ear to the street – a requirement in a Game based on what's new and fresh. These are the people who can do it for you and report while you attend to larger matters. If you treat them poorly, you will lose touch with not only a great resource but you will create a lifelong enemy who will band with other "small people" in an effort to burn you. In The Game, once you lose your roots, you've lost your ability to grow.

You never know who you will meet and where that path will lead them. So, be kind and respectful to all, even the "little people." During the era of the Tastemakers Conferences, I made it a point to welcome everyone and make sure to personally walk in certain guests if their registration process was being delayed. Just this small act of courtesy has rippled forward years later when young, hungry up-and-comers at the time like E. Mackey were so grateful that he decided to look out and create the cover art of this project.

Speaking of the Tastemakers Era, TJ Chapman noted, "we had all types of people that came to the conferences that are now doing big things. Tooma, left MTV Jamz went to Revolt, ran all urban music at Spotify and is now at Youtube. Will Packer was a former DJ in the record pool and now is a big time director and producer in Hollywood, Tubby was at Bad Boy and now is head of Black Music at Sony. If you build the relationships right, and you nurture them and keep up with them, there's no telling how people will grow and become the top dogs of the industry. It's all a relationship thing and it's what people miss."

You never know who someone will grow to be, so be good to everyone.

HOW TO CREATE A RELATIONSHIP

The introduction to a new contact is important. After all, if relationships are the lifeblood of The Game, forming strategic partnerships is the plasma. The partnerships are what make the relationships vital. Remember, people will only rock with you if there is a mutual respect/admiration, if they have something to gain and/or if they get a good vibe from you. In the first interaction, it is important to build some form of chemistry with them. You must treat the person you are talking to as a person. Not as an object.

Understand that introductions can take place at any time, so always stay prepared. The future Temptations met Berry Gordy in the bathroom and flipped that into an audition which eventually got them to be signed to Motown.

Have business cards nearby or your phone handy to exchange information. Also, please consider the environment and surroundings of the introduction. Take into account if it takes place at a club, party or backstage at a concert. The noise levels might be high so sometimes it's best just to greet and exchange information for a follow up encounter. But, meeting a new potential contact in a social environment can also be a good thing. TJ Chapman explains, "going to parties and events…getting around those people in an informal environment when their hair down is the best time to actually build relationships with people."

But, if it happens at a time and place where you can engage in a conversation, do your best to keep it short and sweet while trying to decipher your future relationship's personality. Your goal is to say or do one to two key things so they will keep you positively in mind and connect with them. Usually, this can be done by finding a common ground or eliciting a smile or a laugh. People tend to like you more if you make them smile, make them money and/or you are fun to be around. But, please keep in mind that this is not the time to reveal your best off colored jokes or attempts at trying to get a number for personal reasons. A first impression really does last, so make it a good one. If in doubt, follow Aaron Burr's lead in "Hamilton," talk less and smile more. Your goal should be to make sure they like you enough to encourage another encounter. Yes, you can do business with someone you don't like, but usually the price usually goes up. However for others, they would rather not even be bothered with you. So, keep it friendly and cordial.

If you know who you are speaking to before you are introduced, such as someone with gravitas, find something to compliment such as a successful project they've worked or how you were inspired by them. Even better, ask them a question related to their experiences or expertise. Nothing works better than stroking an ego. Just don't overdo it, nobody likes a suck up.

You should always have something positive to say. Even if what you have to say is negative, frame it constructively and end it with a positive note. People seldom remember what you say, but will often remember how they felt after your conversation.

Now that the introduction is made, it's up to you on what you do with it and how you cultivate it.

CULTIVATING A RELATIONSHIP

Cultivating a relationship is akin to growing a flower. You have to give it some sun and water for it to grow. Or as TJ Chapman puts it, "[people] get the relationship thing twisted because they don't know how to build or nurture them. All these people that I may work with or want to work with or need, no matter how big they are or little, they are people too. So many people neglect that. All they care about is themselves, what they want to achieve or take from that person. The whole approach is unproductive. The biggest thing for me is that it was never about what I needed or what I wanted or what they could do for me. It was about the relationship. Because I always put the relationship first, I didn't even have to talk about the other stuff, because they already knew. It doesn't even need to be said. Don't forget that they are people too. Just like me and you. Stop taking all the time. Give, extend a hand, make it seem like it don't matter. Whatever it was, it was secondary to the relationship."

Once you have their contact information, it is wise to make a personal note that mentions where you met them, who introduced you, or common points of conversation. I have found that writing on the back of a business card or in the note/memo section of a phone contact works best. The purpose is so when you follow up with them, you can refresh their memory of you and your conversation or who introduced you two.

Always ask, "when would be a good time to follow up with you?" This allows you two to enter in a verbal agreement to discuss deeper matters at a future date. It reinforces your communication and when you follow through at the agreed time, it shows your level of professionalism. The higher the level, the more respect you will earn and the more people will want to work with you. Just make sure to actually follow up. This is the precarious part where folks fail. Even if you don't have a particular project per se, you should at least follow up to cement the introduction. If all else fails, just tell them how good it was to meet, thank them for their time and how much you look forward to working with them in the near future. The follow up is what can separate you from the pack, take advantage.

Generally, the people that you meet in The Game are very busy people. If they aren't, they won't be in The Game very long. That means when you reach out to them, make sure you keep it short, simple and to the point with a bit of courtesy because after all, they are still people no matter their status.

Here is an example of a follow up email I used to meet with the director of the school board regarding S.A.B. Fest:

"Hello Ms. Jane [*proper salutation shows respect*], it was a pleasure meeting you the other day with John [*courtesy and you remind them who introduced you*]. I am just following up today as you suggested [*just following their directions, it shows you listen and are professional*] regarding setting up a meeting about the S.A.B. Fest anti-bullying rally [*the reason why you are reaching out to them*]. It would mean the world to meet with you at your earliest convenience to discuss how we can get the schools involved on this important issue. [*demonstrates how important this opportunity is for both of you*]. Late mornings or early afternoons are best for us, but I know your schedule is hectic so what day/time is best for you? [*respectful of their time, call to action and frame a window that they can choose between two yesses*]. Thank you for your time and quick reply [*shows you are respectful of their time and you are humbly asking for a quick answer*],

Keith Kennedy
@KeithK926 | 850.xxx.xxxx [*put your contact info so they can have it at their fingertips. Don't assume they have it handy*]

In the example above, you will notice there are certain subtleties read between the lines of the email. Playing The Game requires a certain amount of finesse. Everything is a move and counter move like chess. If you say or do the wrong thing, nothing happens – a fate that is death in The Game. But, if you hit all the right notes, you will hear the most beautiful sound in The Game -"cha-ching!" A cash register ringing is the winning sound because all of your moves should lead to this one way or the other. Otherwise, you are just building a hobby not a career.

The very best way to cultivate a relationship is through shared experiences. Breaking bread over lunch or dinner, attending an industry function or in a personal case for me, driving around lost in the hood part of Miami for over 45 minutes looking for the best soul food can bond you together and creates a strong relationship. (Kimberly Jo, I see you!) After all, if we can laugh about the situation once, we can laugh forever and thereby become friends, then anything we need of each other will be easily granted.

A great example of utilizing a strong relationship that has been properly cultivated is when I learned DJ Dr. Doom (WJBT-Jacksonville x Official

84

Funkfest DJ) is now the manager for @itskamillion with the hit record, "Twerk 4 Me." DJ Dr. Doom and I have a relationship that goes back years including first and foremost sharing a hometown, then servicing him music through TJ's DJs, then being an attendee to his parties and a fan of his art (he's one of the rare DJs that seems to have more fun at the parties than you) and through shared experiences as a Jaguar season ticket holder. Because of our relationship, when as a club owner I need to book his now rapidly rising new star, we can work out a great price for his artist.

Another example is when I was tasked with finding talent for Blazin' 102.3's Birthday Bash in Tallahassee. One of their artists dropped out at the last minute and now budget and time constraints to begin promotions were tight. After being consulted, I thought it would be a good idea to go after a classic artist that the market would clamor for. Pastor Troy is a legend who came to mind. After a quick call as a personal favor, he was booked under budget and the Program Director, DJ Dap was ecstatic to begin promotions on time with an artist that excited his listeners.

I was able to pull that off because Pastor Troy was appreciative of an article I once wrote about him for OZONE Magazine naming him one of the South's "Top 25 Greatest Artists of All Time." Since that time, we maintained a positive relationship that allowed me to call him like a friend even if we haven't spoken in years.

The good news is that I believe most people inherently *want to help* others. The realistic news is that most people *will only help* others if there is a personal gain involved somewhere down the line. Whether it is for a future favor, financial benefit, or a barter exchange, most people playing The Game inherently ask, "what's in it for them?" Be careful though because as Carlito taught us in "Carlito's Way," "a favor will kill you faster than a bullet."

Your connects have every reason to be self-serving. They worked hard to be in a strong position and never want to be in a situation of giving things away. You will learn that The Game is about leverage. And in this case, you need them more than they need you. To them, giving for nothing is foolish because they know that's not how The Game is played to win. Remember, The Game is won by gaining the equivalent or higher value than whatever you give with every action taken. It is the very definition of profit and loss. Bone Thugs-n-Harmony said it best, "no shorts, no losses."

The question you should have now is; what do I have to offer?

Take stock in what you have. Do you have a hotel hookup, flight connections, or concert tickets? Do you have certain skills or time that is valuable? Everything you have to offer has a certain value. What you are requesting has a value. Now the trick becomes coming to an understanding so both parties benefit. Keep in mind, no one playing The Game is above getting "free" stuff. I've seen free t-shirts cause a frenzy. But in The Game, even free has a value. This Game thrives on the barter system so take advantage.

One great way to build relationships is to be the one that supplies the party favors. TJ had a moniker of "Mr. Happy" because he was the one that always provided the items that helped those around him enjoy themselves. During the Nashville Impact Conference, I brought a bag of focus factor and it endeared me to those that couldn't find it anywhere else. As a result, I became fast friends with new industry heads that are maintained to this day.

If you are to engage in the barter system to build relationships, the most important thing is to always follow through on what you promised then make sure you say thank you and show your appreciation in some manner if they look out for you. A small gift of their favorite bottle, a thank you email / call or better yet a personal card is a nice touch depending on the favor. Remember, they don't have to help, but you should be grateful that they did.

Make sure you keep in contact with your contact. Just touching base from time to time will keep you in the forefront of their mind. Plus, it shows that you care about them as a person not as a hook up.

Another great way to cultivate a relationship is to send little notes of thanks or appreciation during birthdays and holidays. This small gesture can go a long way. Thankfully, Facebook and Google Calendar has a great feature to help keep track of the birthdays of your contacts.

Finally, buying the occasional drink or lunch can help your cause as well. I still remember Quint of New Millenium DJs who once brought in a pizza for the staff or Fran who brought donuts. People in power positions are not above taking tokens in exchange for currying favors or making sure you are the first in mind for an opportunity that they can provide.

DJ Lil Boy offers this nugget, "the best way to cement a relationship is one of three ways. Make money together, [share intimate experiences] or fight together. The emotional bond when you do one of these three things that is formed is unbreakable unless there is a betrayal."

KILLING A RELATIONSHIP

Just as you can build a relationship, you can just as easily kill one.

While it is good to reach out on occasion to check in with your relationship, it is EXTREMELY annoying to be on the receiving end of repetitive, thoughtless messages that are a waste of time. The most terrible is the simple message of "hmu" or "yo," or "I guess you're too good to holla at me now," etc. These messages on their own let its recipients know you don't value their time and you are unable to put together at least two coherent thoughts. Neither of which are good for relationship building. The latter example just implies that you feel they are too good to reach out to you. Even if used in jest, it puts them in a defensive position and also it reminds them why they shouldn't reach out to you when in fact, you should be reaching out to them.

Instead, you should use phrases that keep you positively ingrained in their minds. Because remember, this Game is about relationships and referrals. You want to be first on their minds when they are looking for someone for a particular task, this leads to a gig for you which means more cha-ching!

More favorable follow ups include:

"Hey *NAME*, haven't heard from you in awhile, hope all is well. What's good with you?"

"Hey *NAME*, I heard about your success with the *NAME OF PROJECT*. Congradz! What's next for you?"

The important takeaways are this, use their name when possible. People respond more positively to you when you mention and remember their name (especially when you first meet them. It helps if you use a pneumonic device or word association). Most importantly, it denotes that you aren't spamming them (a strong negative). Plus, you are reaching out to them and it makes them feel like a person that you aren't keeping them around for what they can do for you (even if you are). The question at the end encourages dialog. But, beware in a text message conversation, there should be no more than 2-3 exchanges of dialog and avoid emojis. Anything more than that, you take the risk of becoming annoying and you should have just made it a phone call.

Also, some business is better handled on the phone or in person. Good business relies on being able to read people and without a personal interaction, things may get misconstrued through a simple text message. Text messages cannot detect tone, so you are open to the interpretations of the reader, which depending on the text and the mood of the textee, it may not go well for you.

Another way to kill a relationship is by taking it for granted. In other words, the only time a contact hears from you is when *you* need something. This is why it is so important to nourish the relationship properly. If your contact feels used, the relationship will wither.

Not returning a favor is yet another way a relationship dies. Heard the phrase, scratch my back and I'll scratch yours? If there is no reciprocation and your contact's back remains itchy, then you will forever notice their back as they deliberately turn from you.

Passing along their contact information without prior permission will also kill your relationship. It is an extreme violation for someone unknown to reach out to your contact without them pre-approving or knowing the call is coming. Especially if there is any chance the new people will annoy your contact. If that takes place, you may lose your contact and burn your relationship. If you are unsure, take the time to ask if it is ok for your contact to be contacted by one of your people for x reason. Beyond that, it is just common courtesy. You wouldn't want your information blasted out and have to waste your time with unqualified inquiries. The short solution is your contact doesn't know your people like you do, so make a personal introduction *only* with permission.

Your contacts are valuable because referrals and access are the fundamentals of how you eat. Don't just give them away. That's like leaving a $100 bill in the street for anyone to pick up. It takes time to cultivate these relationships that are the key to your survival. Treat them accordingly.

Finally, one of the quickest ways to kill your relationship is with a breach of trust. If you get caught lying to, messing over or throwing your contact under the bus for any reason prepare for that relationship to die. It's tough to do business with someone who is untrustworthy. How would you feel if you did work with someone but your money never came on time or not at all? How would you feel if every time you were told something, you couldn't judge the veracity of the source? If something were to go wrong and the finger was pointed at you, could you work with the person throwing shade?

Ultimately, the best relationships are long and winding which eventually turns into a true and profitable friendship on both sides. Your goal should be to find, cultivate, and develop as many relationships as possible because that is where your true power will resonate from, thereby giving you best chance to win The Game.

WARNING

Be wary of the Thirsty Connector aka The Name Dropper. This is the one that always adds a famous or influential person in their conversations as if they know them as besties and can always hook you up, but never follow through. They usually are fast talkers and have lines such as, "that time so & so and I did..." or "You don't know so & so, I knew them back when yadda yadda." They are braggadocios people because the truth is, they don't have enough credentials to stand on their own. They are hoping to have shine by association, that is, if they say they know a big timer, then they will be big time in turn. Beware of them, they often cannot fulfill any promises made and odds are that they are trying to make what is at best a casual acquaintance into something that looks good to trap new victims. Keep in mind that connects are currency in The Game, so if someone is that eager to offer their connections, then they weren't that valuable to begin with.

NOTES TO SELF // TODAY I LEARNED ... // MY NEXT STEP IS ...

Pastor Troy Showing Love During & After The Show

10

WHAT TIME IS IT!?…GAME TIME!!

"The game of chess, is like a sword fight..You must think first, before you move"
WU-TANG - *"Da Mystery of Chessboxin'"*

===

"It's time to play the game!"
TRIPLE H (*WWE Superstar***)**

===

"I play my enemies like a game of chess"
LAURYN HILL - *"Ready or Not"*

===

"What time is it!!? ... Game Time!!"
RAY LEWIS (*NFL Hall of Famer***)**

* * *

When you play The Game, it helps to prepare by playing certain games. Then like the movie, "Inception," it becomes The Game within The Game. Why is this important? TJ Chapman explains, "when I was playing Madden, I would get 30 minutes to an hour of their time and build relationships because it was a way to get cool with all of these people. I would go practice so if I beat them I could always call them and talk sh!t."

In fact, we had a travelling Playstation that we took on the road with us and challenged all crews. It created bonding experiences and a chance to build deeper relationships with everyone we played against. I still owe Bo Hagon from the Attic Crew some comeuppance for the way he beat me. Conversely, Fiend (formerly of No Limit) or DJ Nasty (WEDR, 99 Jamz -Miami) never wants any smoke when they come to town. The point is, these are relationships that have gotten deeper over something that was "just a game."

Even though these games can be fun, the underlying current is to use these as a way to bridge the gap of awkwardness between potential contacts and to build relationships. People watch how you play games and will translate that into how you handle business. Do you play with honor, do you cheat, do you throw temper tantrums if The Game goes against you, how do you handle pressure, are you a good sportsman and shake hands at the end? All of this is taken into account when you play these games. Yes, it is fun to win, but win or lose, the important thing is how you play The Game.

There are 6 main games - chess, dominos, video games, spades, tunk, pool (and sometimes dice, but we won't cover that here) that are played by players of The Game. We will go through them and give a few tips and strategies to help you become a better player. Now, I do understand that sometimes experts may place wagers on the games that are played. Although I cannot condone gambling, understand that a fool and their money are soon parted. Do not gamble playing these games if you can't afford to lose. These instructions and tips are for entertainment and relationship building purposes only.

* * *

CHESS

The history of chess can be traced back nearly 1500 years, although the earliest origins are uncertain. The earliest predecessor of the game probably originated in India, before the 6th century AD. From India, the game spread to Persia. When the Arabs conquered Persia, chess was taken up by the Muslim world and subsequently spread to Southern Europe. In Europe, chess evolved into roughly its current form during the 15th century. Today, there are over 600 million daily players around the world.

What makes chess so special? First, it is a game of kings. This game is literally designed to have one king face off against another king for control of a battlefield. Subsequently, the king attempts to use his entire army to defeat the other king knowing that a loss results in death. As such, real life kings used this game as a form to test strategies in war scenarios and to test the mental acuity of his courtesans.

Chess is a thinking and strategy game with millions of move combinations that make each play unique. As Jah Besley puts it, "chess is all about having patience, knowing when to move and when not to; when to be an aggressor or not. It truly is the art of war. A pawn could put you in check or checkmate. The smallest things can end everything that you've been working hard for, so you learn to move different."

Jah continues, "once you pick apart life and business the way you see a chess board, you see things in a different light. You see who are the rooks, knights, bishops, queens and pawns - when to move them, how to move them in certain points in your life. It's not erratic like checkers. Some people you have to sacrifice, some people you have to save. Some people you have to protect. That's how it works, that's how life works. In the end, you have to protect yourself. It sounds selfish, but that's how you learn to elevate to a different place in life."

To summarize the great chess abbot, Rza who declared, in The Game you must "protect yo' neck!"

Here are a few tips to get you started:

LEARN THE MOVES OF EACH PIECE

Each chess piece can move only in a certain way and can be taken only when an opposing piece lands on the same square. For instance, a pawn moves straight ahead one square at a time (unless on an opening move when they can move two spaces) but can only attack on an angle. A knight's move is L-shaped, allowing it to "jump" pieces in an always two by one square format. The bishop moves at an angle with as many squares as it wants as long as it is unimpeded - one moves only on black squares, the other on white. The rook (castle) can move as many squares as necessary but only in a straight line forward, back or to the side. The queen, the most powerful piece, can move in any direction for any number of squares, but not two directions in one move. The king moves at a stately pace — as a king should — one square at a time in any direction. But, two kings cannot occupy border squares at the same time.

OPEN WITH A PAWN

Move the pawn in front of either the king or queen two squares forward. (Once again, only on its opening move can a pawn move two squares). This opens pathways for your bishops and queen to enter the game. They move on an angle and can't get out onto the field of battle if pawns are in the way. As you get better, there are strategies to get the queen out quickly that puts strong pressure on your opponent that can make them fold quickly.

GET THE KNIGHTS AND BISHOPS OUT

Before you move your queen, rooks or king, move your knights and bishops toward the center of the board. You want to get these pieces out from behind the pawns so they can attack. Sometimes it is wise to get the knights out before your pawns to keep the centerfield under control.

KEEP YOUR HEAD ON A SWIVEL

When it's your turn, always think to yourself, "What did my opponent's last move do? What is he up to?" Is he laying traps to capture my pieces? Then decide on your own plan. Always look at *ALL* of your possibilities. Look at moves that would capture your opponent's pieces or threaten his king first. But always double-check your moves before you play them. Ask yourself, "Does my move leave a piece unprotected?" Remember, a move doesn't officially count until you take your hand off of the moved piece.

DON'T WASTE TIME

Don't make too many moves with your pawns or try to pick off your opponent's pawns unless it serves a greater purpose. As in The Game, stay away from petty squabbles and keep your eye on the bigger picture.

"CASTLE" EARLY

Castling is a move that allows you to move your king to safety and bring your rook into play. Once all the squares between your rook and the king are unoccupied you can move the king two squares toward the rook while the rook moves to the square on the king's other side. If your opponent neglects to castle, you might be able to launch an attack on his king. This is the only move in which more than one piece may be moved in a turn.

ATTACK IN THE "MIDDLE GAME"

After you've brought all your knights and bishops into the game and castled (these moves are your "opening"), the middle game begins. In the middle game, always be on the lookout for ways to capture your opponent's pieces. Take any piece that your opponent doesn't protect. But, look at what will happen to your piece if you take his — will you get picked off? Always be looking for ways to move your men into position to attack the enemy king.

Understand and anticipate the consequences of each move before you make it.

LOSE PIECES WISELY

You'll take some of your opponent's pieces. Some of your pieces will be taken. You must figure out what is and isn't a good swap. Use these points that are assigned in tournament play to figure out whether you're making a good move if you're going to lose one of them:

- Queen: 9 points
- Rook: 5 points
- Bishop: 3 points
- Knight: 3 points
- Pawn: 1 point

KING · K   QUEEN · Q   BISHOP · B   KNIGHT · N   ROOK · R   PAWN · P

shutterstock.com · 1874314126

So is it a good idea to lose a bishop to save a pawn? No!

DON'T PLAY TOO FAST

If you see a good move, sit on your hands and look for a better one. Patient thinking is the key to chess success. Make your next move, your best move.

WIN THE ENDGAME

After you and your opponent swap pieces and you're down to just a few remaining, the end game begins. Now the pawns become more important. If you can advance a pawn to the farthest row away from you, that pawn becomes a queen. Everyone's gotta have a dream! Let your king attack, too, as long as he stays out of reach of your opponent's remaining pieces — especially the queen — and does not lend himself to be checked. However, the two kings are not allowed to directly attack each other.

Your king is said to be in check when your opponent threatens to use one of his pieces to capture the king on his next move. If your king is checked and you have no way to remove the threat — it can't run away, you can't capture the opposing piece that has him in check and you can't block the check by moving one of your own pieces — the game is lost. Checkmate! If you checkmate your opponent before he checkmates you, then you win! If neither player can capture the king with the remaining pieces on the board, it is a stalemate or draw.

* * *

DOMINOS

As mentioned by Ice Cube on "Today Was A Good Day," Dominos is a tile based game played with rectangular "domino" tiles. Each domino is a rectangular tile with a line dividing its face into two square ends. Each end is marked with a number of spots (also called pips, nips, or dobs) or is blank. The backs of the dominos in a set are indistinguishable, either blank or having some common design. The domino gaming pieces make up a domino set, sometimes called a deck or pack. The traditional Sino-European domino set consists of 28 dominoes, featuring all combinations of spot counts between zero and six.

The earliest mention of dominos is from the Song Dynasty in China as found in the text "Former Events in Wulin" by Zhou Mi (1232–1298). Modern dominos first appeared in Italy during the 18th century, but how Chinese dominos developed into the modern game is unknown. Italian missionaries in China may have brought the game to Europe. In fact, the name "domino" is most likely from the resemblance to a kind of carnival costume worn during the Venetian Carnival, often consisting of a black-hooded robe and a white mask.

European-style dominoes are traditionally made of bone or ivory (hence the game's nickname, "bones"), or a dark hardwood such as ebony, with contrasting black or white pips (inlaid or painted). Alternatively, domino sets have been made from many different natural materials: stone, wood, metals, ceramic clay, frosted glass or crystal. These sets have a more novel look, and the often heavier weight makes them feel more substantial; also, such materials and the resulting products are usually much more expensive than polymer materials.

The traditional set of dominos contains one unique piece for each possible combination of two ends with zero to six spots, and is known as a double-six set because the highest-value piece has six pips on each end (the "double six"). The spots from one to six are generally arranged as they are on six-sided dice, but because blank ends having no spots are used, seven faces are possible, allowing 28 unique pieces in a double-six set.

HOW TO PLAY DOMINOS

First, you must determine which style you are playing. There are two main types. One, where the players put down matching tiles and when the ends total 5, points are awarded and the one with the most points wins.

But, the second and by far the most popular with those that play The Game is the one we will be discussing here – Last One Standing. Although this game can be played between 2-4 players, for the purpose of this guide, we will assume there are 4. The only difference is that if there are fewer than 4, the remaining tiles will be placed in a pool that the players draw from if they don't have any matching tiles in their hand when they "knock."

1. Start with all dominos facing down on the table. Shuffle or "wash" all of the dominoes in a circular motion.

2. Each player draws 7 tiles from the pool.

3. For the first round, the player with the Double 6 tile plays first.

4. Each player starting from the 1st player's left takes turns to match the tiles that are face up on the table.

5. If a player cannot match a tile, then they must "knock" and pass their turn.

6. Rounds continue until the player empties their hand and with the last tile slams it on the table and like Ice Cube, start "yellin' 'domino!!'." Then you can do a victory celebration. That player is now the first in the next game after all the tiles have been placed faced down and washed again. (Bonus points if nobody you know got killed in South Central, LA.)

7. If the game is "locked" and no players are able to match the available tiles, then all players must show the remaining tiles in their hand and the player with the least amount of total dots, wins.

STRATEGIES FOR BEGINNERS

1. The one that plays first has the advantage until they knock. Then it goes to the next player on their left.

2. There are 7 faces of each domino side. Play accordingly.

3. If you have multiple tiles with the same number combination, do your best to book end the game so you can force knocking from other players.

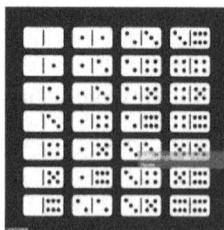

VIDEO GAMES

There are thousands of video game titles across several platforms, but the most popular games that are played within The Game are Madden and NBA 2K. Although, Call of Duty is big online and you may catch an occasional gamer rapper such as Big K.R.I.T. in a lobby near you. Make no mistake, although these are games, the competition is very real. If you are not good at these games, the only way you will get better is with practice. Play at home if you must, online if you can, but get better through game play. If you can hold your own, you will gain a level of respect that can't be bought.

These games are about reflexes and understanding the nuances of how each computer player moves, with and without the ball. The plays you call and the way you execute them under pressure situations are what can separate victory from defeat. When in doubt, pick the best team with the best players until you find a team that fits your style. Although, in some circles this can be seen as a weak move, do everything you can to get an advantage. Especially, if you explain that you are new to this. Just do your best to not get skunked, 21-0. Then you will be kicked off the sticks in disgrace.

2Pac (l) Playing Video Games With Suge Knight (r)

SPADES

The history of Spades can be tracked to some similar card games, played 100 years ago. It is assumed it descended from Bid Whist. Spades also has a kindred spirit with Bridge, Pinochle, Euchre and other similar games featuring partnership play, bidding and a trump suit.

George Coffin, the great Bridge author, traced the roots of Spades to sometime between 1937 and 1939. Spades was played extensively during

World War II as it was a fast paced game, which could be interrupted at any time – especially convenient during battle conditions!

The modern game of Spades became popular in the late 1940's, especially on college campuses. It is difficult to pinpoint a single creator of the game. It is believed it was invented by US students who enjoyed both Bid Whist and Bridge. They were looking for a fast-paced game that was competitive and strategic. The roots of the game can be traced back to the Mid-West. It is determined that this game was introduced first in Cincinnati, Ohio, among the student society.

The traditional card deck that everyone is familiar with originated from the Latin suits. The Latin suits consisted of swords (spades), cups (hearts), coins (diamonds) and clubs. They each represented the nobility, clergymen, merchant and peasant classes.

The word "Spades" is a loan from the Italian spade, meaning "swords." The English borrowed the French visual forms from the traditional French playing cards, which don't particularly look like swords, but, by pure coincidence, do look a bit like the digging implements known as "spades."

Shout out to E. Mackey for bringing a new urban flavor to this classic game. Check out www.blvckspades.com to pick up your own signature deck.

STYLES OF PLAY

There are two styles of play when it comes to spades. Traditional and The Hood Way. We will cover the Hood Way which is will be the more popular version in your travels.

THE HOOD WAY

First, the jokers are inserted and the 2 of clubs and 2 of hearts are removed.

The order of dominance is Big Joker (usually the colored one), Little Joker (the black & white one), 2 of Diamonds, 2 of Spades, A, K, Q, J, 10-3.

The dealer shuffles and after the player to their right cuts the cards issues everyone 13 cards beginning on the dealer's left. The game play is the same as the traditional, save for the order mentioned above and there is no pre-bidding. Scoring is done by awarding one point for every book earned by the team after the 7th. So, if your team won 9 books for that hand, they earned 2 points. The first team to 7 points wins. If a team wins 13 books also known as "running a Boston," the game is automatically over. And massive amounts of sh!t talking will commence.

TIPS

1. It ain't over til it's over. The card gods are a fickle beast. They may be against you one hand and give you the perfect set the next. Hang in there!

2. Always watch the board and pay attention to what your partner is playing. You two must have good synergy to keep your opponents at bay. This is what Jay-Z was looking for in "Excuse Me Miss," "a partner to play spades with / the cards up, all trumps."

3. This game above all has the most trash talk barbs traded. Don't take it personally and learn to fire shots of your own. Just be mindful to walk the line between light ribbing and below the belt jabs.

4. Learn how to count the cards of a suit and understand the probability of who has what so you can anticipate the proper plays. And make sure you don't renege by playing the proper suits in the wrong order. You will then be subject to the loss of three books and massive amounts of respect.

5. Make sure you call straight cuts and straight deals. When you play the hood way, sometimes they like to flip cards and do different techniques

to gain advantages.

* * *

TUNK

Tonk, or tunk, is a matching card game, which combines features of gin rummy and conquian. Tonk is a relatively fast paced game that can be played by 2-4 players. It was popular with blues and jazz musicians in southern Louisiana in the 1930s, including Duke Ellington's orchestra, and was played during breaks in the back rooms of bars and saloons. In many other places it has become a popular pastime for workers while on their lunch breaks.

HOW TO PLAY

Players are dealt five, seven, or nine cards, depending on the number of players, in turn. The dealer turns up the first of the un-dealt cards as the start of the discard pile. Some people play that the dealer does not turn up the first card. The discard pile is started after the first player draws. The remaining un-dealt cards are set face down in a stack next to the discard pile. These form the stock.

The goal of play is to get rid of one's cards by forming them into spreads. A spread is three or four identical cards (such as three 5's or four Queens), or three or more in a row of the same suit. A player may add cards to his own or another's spread. The winner is the first to get rid of all his cards, or the player with the fewest points when play is stopped.

Play stops when a player gets rid of all his cards, or when a player "drops" by laying his cards face up on the table. A player may drop at any point in the

103

game (some play you can only drop before drawing), including right after the cards are dealt. When a player drops, all the players likewise lay their cards face up. The player with the fewest points in his hand is the winner.

If the player does not drop, he must take a card from the top or one under from the discard pile or from the stock. The player may then lay face up any spreads, or add to any spreads on the table. If after this the player has no more cards, he says, "tonk" and wins.

If the player has one or more cards remaining, he must discard one card to the discard pile. If this is his last card, play ends. He is the winner. If the player has one or more cards left in his hand after discarding, his turn ends.

If the stock runs out, play stops. The player with the fewest points in his hand wins. If two or more players tie the hand is a draw, and another hand is dealt.

Many variations in play are possible.

MELDING

Players can meld sets (three of the same rank card) or runs (three consecutive cards in the same suit, e.g.: 9 10 J), but may not "bridge the gap" by melding K A 2. Yet, aces may be played as high or low card.

HITTING

Hitting is a variation of the common laying off of another player's meld (i.e.: you hit an opponent's set of three 10s with the other 10). The card is put with the melds of the player who is receiving the hit. However, when a player "hits" another player, the player receiving the hit cannot lay down for one turn. Multiple hits result in additional loss of lay downs for turns thereafter. After a player has hit another player, the hitting player is allowed to discard a card from his hand. Once a player's set has been hit and the four cards of

104

that rank are melded, they can be thrown into the discard pile. You cannot spread out.

* * *

POOL

The game of billiards a.k.a. pool has a long and rich history. It's been played by kings, commoners, presidents, mental patients, ladies, gentlemen and hustlers alike. Billiards began as a lawn game similar to the croquet played sometime during the 15th century in Northern Europe. It has evolved from that point into the present-day style of billiard/pool table and rules.

The game moved indoors to a wooden table with green cloth to simulate grass and a simple border around the edges. The term "billiard" is derived from the French language, either from the word "billart," one of the wooden sticks, or "bille," a ball. Shakespeare even mentioned it in his play, "Antony & Cleopatra."

In the original game players would turn a mace around and use its handle to strike the ball. The handle was called a "queue" meaning "tail" from which we get the word "cue." Billiard/pool tables originally had flat walls for rails and their only function was to keep the balls from falling off. They used to be called "banks" because they slightly resembled the banks of a river. Billiard players discovered that the balls could bounce off the rails and began deliberately aiming at them, and therefore the "bank shot" was born!

The talent of a professional pool player is truly amazing! Visitors from England showed Americans how the use of spin can make the billiard ball behave differently depending on what type and amount of spin you put on the ball, which explains why it is called "English" in the United States but nowhere else. The British themselves refer to it as "side."

HOW TO PLAY

Familiarize yourself with the equipment. There are generally three things you'll be using: a cue stick, table, and pool balls.

Pick a cue stick appropriate for your size. Most are 58 inches (147 cm) in length, but shorter and longer ones are available. The tip is the most important part of a cue (it's on the narrow end you'll be hitting with). Tips vary from soft to hard, though inexperienced pool players are best served with a medium to medium-soft tip. And there are three standard sizes to a pool table: 7, 8, and 9 feet (2.7 m).

As for the pool balls, there are evens and odds, solids and stripes, and, most importantly, the 8 ball and the cue ball. The cue ball is solid white, a bit heavier, and should be the only ball directly hit during the game.

Learn the language. In order to play the game, you have to be able to understand the terminology and rules. Familiarizing yourself with the vocabulary of the game will make it easier and quicker to learn. Let's stick to the standard and more popular 8-ball rules.

Use the triangle to "rack up" the 15 pool balls. Different people have different preferences for the set up, but make sure the 8-ball is in the middle.

The "break" happens at the beginning of the game when a player breaks up the fifteen pool balls. It is the first shot. Some players break straight on while others break at an angle. If he or she makes a ball into a pocket, he or she claims that type (solid or stripes also known as "hi" or "low" respectively) for the duration of the game and shoots again. The other player receives the variation they did not claim. If the player makes a ball of each variation, they may choose which one they prefer.

A scratch occurs when the cue ball jumps off the table or rolls into a pocket.

Determine the scratch rules before you start any game. It is common for the player who did not receive the scratch to be allowed to place the cue ball anywhere in the "kitchen" upon their subsequent turn. This is the area between the edge and the second set of diamonds denoted on the rail. Although some play a variation that allows a "ball-in-hand" approach that allows the player to place the cue ball anywhere on the table for their turn after the other player scratches.

Both players sink all their pool balls into the pockets until just the 8 ball is left. The first player to sink the 8 ball is the winner. If a player inadvertently sinks a ball of the other player's, it counts to the other player's benefit. If a player inadvertently sinks the 8 ball before all their other balls are in, they lose. If a player scratches on the 8 ball, they automatically lose as well.

MASTER THE STROKE

Each person has a different preferred hand position. If you are right-handed, hold the base of the stick with your right hand and rest the narrow end on your left. If you are left-handed, do the opposite.

For a good hand position, try putting your index finger on the top of the stick (curving it) and put your thumb at the bottom of the stick. This is a good, basic way to put your hand in position because you have total control of the stick. Hold it tight as well. Some will prefer to rest the stick on their index finger while others may rest the cue in between their fingers in a flatter style. Experiment with a few to see what yields the best results. This hand will never move. Only move your back arm when shooting. Your feet should be a little wider than shoulder-width apart and at a 45-degree angle.

During your practice strokes, your eyes should switch from the contact point on the cue ball to the point you're aiming for on the object ball. Make the shots. Line the pool tip up with the cue ball, aim, and hit away! As a beginner, focus on hitting the cue ball straight and with power. Aim as if you were to directly hit your object ball. See that spot you'd be hitting if you were allowed to? Alright. Now, aim to get the cue ball to *that spot* on your object ball. Experiment with slow, easy shots. Sometimes a softer touch helps your ball to ride the edge of the table or stay in a more defensive position.

* * *

NOTES TO SELF // TODAY I LEARNED ... // MY NEXT STEP IS ...

11

I HAVE THE POWER

"I have the power!"
HE-MAN

===

"With great power comes great responsibility."
UNCLE BEN, *"Spider Man"*

===

"Power tends to corrupt, and absolute power corrupts absolutely. Great men are almost always bad men."
SIR JOHN DALBERG-ACTON, *8th Baronet*

* * *

Power is defined as the ability to do something or act in a particular way; or the capacity or ability to direct or influence the behavior of others or the course of events. In other words, power is the ability to do what you want, when you want and to whom you want at your desire.

Power is a very dangerous element. It is something that we all crave because being powerless is a feeling no one wants to experience. Disgraced Hollywood producer, Harvey Weinstein is proof of what happens when absolute power corrupts absolutely. He was convicted and sentenced to 23 years in prison for using his power as one of the top decision makers in entertainment to take advantage of women attempting to advance their careers.

Conversely, after being powerless while in prison for 27 years, Nelson Mandela emerged stronger than ever and was elected president of his native South Africa. Despite temptation to punish those that wronged him, he used his power to unite and made his country whole.

When you have the power in your hands, what will you do with it? The choice is yours.

As the French author, Honore de Balzac wrote and was quoted in the movie, "The Godfather," "behind every great fortune there is a crime." In order to win and obtain power at the highest levels of The Game, you must sometimes break the established rules to survive and ascend. The Kennedy fortune was amassed through bootlegging, William Randolph Hearst started wars to sell newspapers, Henry Ford sold to both sides of world wars, Carnegie terrorized unions, and even Jay-Z was a dope dealer. But, "Hov did that so hopefully you wouldn't have to go through that." Make sure the good ultimately outweighs the bad and be prepared to suffer any consequences of poor decisions. Once you make it, however, walk a righteous path or the past will come back to get you. Only then will the ends justify the means.

Choose your path wisely because power is like sand. Just when you think you have it in your hands, it slips through your fingers.

Robert Greene wrote the definitive book about power, simply titled "The 48 Laws of Power." Since it is such a perfect description on how to gain, wield and lose power, I have made a summary of the key points. Although, it is highly recommend you read the book in its entirety. It is the first book TJ made me read when I broke into the industry as an intern and I suggest you do the same.

Never outshine the master

Make your masters appear more brilliant than they are and you will attain the heights of power. The power behind the throne can wield great results. But when it comes to power, outshining the master is perhaps the worst mistake of all. You must always keep your ego in check, never take your position for granted and never let any favors you give/receive go to your head or you will lose yours by the master.

Never put too much trust in friends, learn how to use enemies

Hire a former enemy and he will be more loyal than a friend, because he has more to prove. In fact, you have more to fear from friends than from enemies. If you have no enemies, find a way to make them. They will keep you sharp. Your friends will rarely be honest because they don't want to hurt your feelings if they disagree with you. As a result, you may never know how a friend truly feels. Friends will say that they love your cooking, adore your music, envy your taste in clothes— maybe they mean it, often they do not.

The key to power, then, is the ability to judge who is best able to further your interests in all situations. Keep friends for friendship, but work only with the skilled and competent.

Conceal Your Intentions

Use decoys, false desires and red herrings to throw people off the scent. Hide your intentions not by closing up (with the risk of appearing secretive, and making people suspicious) but by talking endlessly about your desires and goals— just not your real ones.

You will kill three birds with one stone: You appear friendly, open, and trusting; you conceal your intentions; and you send your rivals on time-consuming wild goose chases.

Use smoke screens to disguise your actions. This derives from a simple truth: people can only focus on one thing at a time. It is really too difficult for them to imagine that the bland and harmless person they are dealing with is simultaneously setting up something else. PT Barnum (founder, Barnum & Bailey Circus) demonstrated that the world wants to be deceived.

Always say less than necessary

Those that cannot control their words shows that he cannot control himself, and is unworthy of respect. But the human tongue is a beast that few can master. It strains constantly to break out of its cage, and if it is not tamed, it will run wild and cause you grief. Power cannot accrue to those who squander their treasure of words.

Power is in many ways a game of appearances, and when you say less than necessary, you inevitably appear greater and more powerful than you are.

Learn the lesson: Once the words are out, you cannot take them back. Keep them under control. Be particularly careful with sarcasm. The momentary satisfaction you gain with your biting words will be outweighed by the price you pay.

So much depends on reputation, guard it with your life

Always be alert to potential attacks and thwart them before they happen. Meanwhile, learn to destroy your enemies by opening holes in their own reputations. Then stand aside and let public opinion hang them.

Doubt is a powerful weapon. Once you let it out of the bag with insidious rumors, your opponents are in a horrible dilemma. If you have a solid base of respect, ridiculing your opponent puts him on the defensive and draws more attention to you, enhancing your own reputation.

Get others to do the work for you, but always take the credit

Credit and therefore the power goes to those that claim it. Be careful as they are also the first to get blamed if it goes badly. Keep your hands clean and always have a scapegoat readily available.

Make other people come to you, use bait if necessary

For negotiations or meetings, it is always wise to lure others into your territory, or one of your choosing. You have your bearings, while they see nothing familiar and are subtly placed on the defensive. If you choose the battle ground, you have a decided advantage.

Win through your actions, never through argument

Actions will always speak louder than words.

Learn to keep people dependent on you

If people are depending on you, they will do everything they can to keep you strong because their survival is dependent upon it.

When asking for help, appeal to people's self-interest, never their mercy or gratitude

People as a general whole want to help, but only inasmuch as to how they will benefit in the end.

Pose as a friend, work as a spy

If you come in as a friend with kindness and understanding, they will tell you everything you need to know. Take notes for you will never know when it will be time to use this information to your advantage.

Strike the shepherd and the sheep will scatter / Crush your enemy totally

Within any group, trouble can most often be traced to a single source, the unhappy, chronically dissatisfied one who will always stir up dissension and infect the group with his or her ill ease. Before you know what hit you, the dissatisfaction spreads. Act before it becomes impossible to disentangle. Once you recognize who the stirrer is, pointing it out to other people will accomplish a great deal and if you are in a position to terminate them, do so without hesitation. Just be sure to eviscerate your enemy as a warning to others and so there will be nothing that can come back to seek vengeance.

Use absence to increase strength and re-invention

The more you are seen and heard from, the more common you appear. In entertainment, strength is gained by the ability to be desired yet inaccessible. You must create value through scarcity. Additionally, if you wish to reinvent yourself, you must disappear for a time to have the old image of you flushed. Then burst on the scene with the new version of you to gain a new power. A temporary withdrawal will make you more talked about and admired. Learn when to leave.

Do not build a fortress to protect yourself, isolation is dangerous.

When you become an island upon yourself, no one will be there to help or guard you and you will be powerless. Rather, build a strong team to further your cause. Keep things vague and simple yet sensational while setting up an us vs them group dynamic to achieve the best results.

Know who you're dealing with, do not offend the wrong person

If you make enemies with the wrong person, you may not be a match. Do your research before you decide who to target. And most importantly, never underestimate your opponent.

Do not commit to anyone

Stay out of other people's business unless you can see an advantage in jumping into the fray. You have a finite amount of energy and resources. Only make a move on someone's behalf if it will benefit you in the long run.

Play a sucker to catch a sucker, seem dumber than your mark

Given how important the idea of intelligence is to most people's vanity, it is critical to never inadvertently insult or impugn a person's brain power. Plus, when you appear less than your victim, they will be so busy trying to scheme they will tell you everything that you want to know.

Enter action with boldness

Fortune favors the bold. When you are as small and obscure as David was, you must find a Goliath to attack. The larger the target, the more attention you gain - such as 50 Cent vs Ja Rule. Move with strength and purpose or as Notorious B.I.G. stated on "Sky's The Limit," "don't make a move unless your hearts in it."

Plan all the way to the end

Always have the end game in mind as you move. That way everything you do will be towards that purpose.

Make your accomplishments seem effortless, yet never appear too perfect

If you make it look easy, it attracts others. When they attempt to do what you do and can't, they will have a new respect for you. Initially, they will imitate and you may take offense. However, this is the most sincere form of flattery. Be mindful that envy creates silent enemies. It is smart to occasionally display defects, and admit to harmless vices, in order to deflect envy and appear more human and approachable. Do not try to help or do favors for those who envy you; they will think you are condescending to them.

Control the options, get others to play with the cards you deal

When you dictate the choices of a situation, you control the board. Even as the illusion of choice remains in their mind.

Color The Choices: Propose three or four choices of action for each situation, and present them in such a way that the one you preferred always seemed the best solution compared to the others.

Force The Resister: Push them to "choose" what you want them to do by appearing to advocate the opposite. Alter the playing field.

The Shrinking Options: A variation on this technique is to raise the price every time the buyer hesitates and another day goes by. This is an excellent negotiating ploy to use on the chronically indecisive, who will fall for the idea that they are getting a better deal today than if they wait till tomorrow.

The Weak Man On The Precipice: This tactic is similar to "Color the Choices," but with the weak you have to be more aggressive. Work on their emotions —use fear and terror to propel them into action. Try reason and they will always find a way to procrastinate.

Brothers In Crime: You attract your victims to some criminal scheme, creating a bond of blood and guilt between you.

The Horns of A Dilemma: The lawyer leads the witnesses to decide between two possible explanations of an event, both of which poke a hole in their story. They have to answer the lawyer's questions, but whatever they say they hurt themselves. The key to this move is to strike quickly - deny the victim the time to think of an escape. As they wriggle between the horns of the dilemma, they dig their own grave.

Discover each man's thumbscrew

Everyone has a weakness, a gap in the castle wall. That weakness is usually an insecurity, an uncontrollable emotion or need; it can also be a small secret pleasure. Either way, once found, it is a thumbscrew you can turn to your advantage.

Pay attention to gestures and unconscious signals. Look for contrasts, an overt trait often reveals its opposite. Find the weak link. Fill their emotional void. Feed on their uncontrollable emotion. Always look for passions and obsessions that cannot be controlled. What people cannot control, you can control for them.

Be royal in your own fashion. Act like a king to be treated like one

People will treat you as you carry yourself. So act accordingly.

Master the art of timing

Everything happens in its time, but you must be prepared and know when to strike. NFL & FSU Hall of Famer Deion Sanders teaches, "if you stay ready, you won't have to get ready."

Disdain things you cannot have, ignoring them is the best revenge

Remember: You choose to let things bother you. You can just as easily

117

choose not to notice the irritating offender, to consider the matter trivial and unworthy of your interest. That is the powerful move.

Desire often creates paradoxical effects: The more you want something, the more you chase after it, the more it eludes you. The more interest you show, the more you repel the object of your desire. This is because your interest is too strong— it makes people awkward, even fearful. Uncontrollable desire makes you seem weak, unworthy, pathetic. Focus on what you can control and let everything else come to you.

Control your emotions

Anger and emotion are strategically counterproductive. You must always stay calm and objective. But if you can make your enemies angry while staying calm yourself, you gain a decided advantage.

Do not go past the mark you aimed for. In victory, know when to stop

Once you have won the battle or received the answer you want, end it and let it be done. If you push too far, you may destroy the gains you made. Billy Beane in the movie, "Moneyball" said it best, "when you get the answer you want, hang up the phone."

Assume formlessness

By taking a shape, by having a visible plan, you open yourself to attack. Instead of taking a form for your enemy to grasp, keep yourself adaptable, unpredictable and on the move. Accept the fact that nothing is certain and no law is fixed. The best way to protect yourself is to be as fluid and formless as water; never bet on stability or lasting order. Everything changes.

* * *

NOTES TO SELF // TODAY I LEARNED ... // MY NEXT STEP IS ...

12

TAKE ME TO YOUR LEADER

"Uneasy lies the head that wears a crown."
HENRY IV, *William Shakespeare's Henry IV, Part 2*

===

"Do not follow where the path may lead. Go instead where there is no path and leave a trail."
RALPH WALDO EMERSON *(Poet)*

===

"Don't tell people how to do things, tell them what to do and let them surprise you with their results."
GENERAL GEORGE PATTON *(US Army)*

===

"Be strong enough to stand alone, smart enough to know when you need help, and brave enough to ask for it."
UNKNOWN

===

"A leader is a dealer in hope."
NAPOLEON BONAPARTE *(French Commander)*

===

"Alone we can do so little; together we can do so much."
HELEN KELLER *(Author x Activist)*

* * *

Teamwork makes the dream work. Since you will not be able to rise very far in The Game without a strong team to support you, at some point you will have to take on a leadership role. If this makes you uncomfortable, that is good. The uneasy feeling will keep you sharp and on edge to make sure your decision making is on point for your team. Analyze all sides of a decision, trust your instincts and figure out the right path. Then go all out and correct accordingly along the way. Just make sure you never let your troops ever, EVER, _EVER_ see you second guessing the moves you make.

Doubt leaves an opening to where they will question your moves leading to an erosion of their confidence in you. Their trust in you as a leader will be gone. You will lose all ability to get anything accomplished until you do something dramatic to earn back their respect or be forced to fire them all and start over. Mickey Pearson in the movie, "The Gentleman" says it best, "if you wish to be king of the jungle, it's not enough. You must BE the king. There can be no doubt, because doubt causes chaos and one's demise."

What makes an effective leader? A leader is one that can do the hard thing while bringing a group together to focus them on a specific goal or task. In this context, it sounds rather simple. However, being a leader can be very difficult and stressful. You are the one others rely on to make the hard decisions. You are the one they come to for every problem, so you must always have an answer or solution. You are the one that has to manage and merge personalities. You are the one that has to come up with the plan or at least the proper way to execute the plan. You are the one that has to pivot when things invariably go wrong. And when it does, you are the one that gets the blame and possibly some credit when things go right. But at the end of the day, even with all of the pressures and knowing it is often a thankless task, you can go home with a smile if the task is done well. Because as Zakiya Alta Lee explains, "a group of people coming together as a team for a common goal is super exiting!"

In my time, I have been led and I have taken the lead. Both roles are equally important on your road to success. However, according to DJ Dap, "before you can be a leader, you must learn to be a follower and you have to do your job well, no matter what." In this way, you can be a team player learning what works or doesn't without putting your neck on the line. Then when it is your turn to take the mantle, you can be better prepared by scoping what was effective or not from the previous team leader.

When it is your turn to be a leader, understand that your survival depends on how well you coach your team. Legendary Hall of Fame UCLA college basketball coach, John Wooden stated, "success is peace of mind which is a direct result of self-satisfaction in knowing you made the best effort to become the best." A good leader will bring out the best in their team, while the best leaders take them beyond what they realize they are capable of.

Wooden has 12 amazing leadership lessons that we will go into now.

1. *Good Values Attract Good People*
   People want to be on a team that are fighting for a good cause. If you propose a high quality mission and environment, high quality people will want to join in. Especially if it is a winning team.

2. *Love Is The Most Powerful Four Letter Word*
   The movie "Monsters Inc." taught us that laughing and love can power a city much better than fear ever could.

3. *Call Yourself A Teacher*
   If you are able to educate as well as lead, you will be revered and more satisfied in what you are doing because you are changing lives. Not just using the team to get you to a certain point.

4. *Emotion Is Your Enemy*
   While you play The Game you will come across many unexpected twists and turns. If your team is afraid of triggering your emotional outbursts, then they will lose respect, withhold information for self-preservation or take other self-protective measures that will impede success.

5. *It Takes 10 Hands To Make A Basket*
   Everyone on the team must contribute for all to be successful.

6. *Little Things Make Big Things Happen*
   The mundane, day-to-day tasks are what eventually allow for the breakthroughs to take place. Each year the Colorado River coursed its way through rock at a rate of the thickness of a sheet of paper. Millions of years later, the Grand Canyon now exists as a natural wonder of the world. The little made the big thing happen.

7. *Make Each Day Your Masterpiece*
   You have 24 hours per day to do what you need to do. If you make each day the best one by doing everything possible to get the best out of it, eventually your team will accomplish everything you set forth.

8. *The Carrot Is Mightier Than A Stick*
   It is better to motivate through tangible rewards than through fear and punishment.

9. *Make Greatness Attainable By All*
   This is a team effort and if everyone has a chance at greatness, then they will do everything possible to attain their portion of it.

10. *Seek Significant Change*
    Nothing great occurs by seeking the status quo. Go after the big change to change your life!

11. *Don't Look At The Scoreboard*
    It ain't over til it's over. If you are watching or keeping track of the score during The Game, you will miss out on the plays you need to execute to win The Game.

12. *Adversity Is Your Asset*
    The entrepreneur sees possibility in every issue. Use the hard thing to your advantage and it will make you stronger.

TJ Chapman states that "one of the keys to my success is that I've always had a dope team. The [Wildstyle] stores, K Camp, B.o.B, Trap ... it's the team! The people there that are there to support you make all the difference in the world. Many people are scared of the team. They won't pick people that aren't as smart as them because they will feel less intimidated. Sh!t, that ain't how you win! I'll take the time to train and help them understand and grow to help them get better."

TAKING CARE OF YOUR PEOPLE

"I treat my men good, but not too good, or I'm not needed. I give just enough so that they need me, but they don't hate me."
SONNY, *"A Bronx Tale"*

===

Jah offers the following warning, "all the employees have a structure. The minute they become aware and start asking what you are taking home, they are not focused on making the business grow, they are worried about others and not making the business grow. Then it becomes something else, I can't give you more because the business will fail. It will take away from other obligations."

It would be nice if your team were there for the love of the mission and not the love of money. There are times when this does happen. In fact, during my TJ's DJs and Wildstyle days, at first coming to work was amazing so the check was secondary. Then the real world kicked in and eventually there were extra bills to pay. So pay structure became more important. Eventually, your people will have to choose a path that makes the most financial sense to them. Consequently, make sure you take care of your people to the best your budget allows. After all, this is still a business designed to turn a profit. To keep retention and morale high, make sure your team feels valued and whenever possible, show them that they are appreciated for their hard work.

TJ would get the staff a massage on occasion or we would go out to staff dinners paid for by the company. These days at The Venue, I make sure to pay the staff extra whenever we have a good night plus let them finish off any refreshments to encourage them and to reduce the urge to steal. If your staff feels undervalued, they will find a way to make it up somehow, usually at your expense and without your knowledge. But, if they have a chance to grow with the company and their boat rises with the tides of the organization, their loyalty will be unwavering. Present options that include a chance for them to win personally if they bring additional business. It is better to give them a small percentage than to have 100% of nothing. You win regardless as business increases and your people will be eager to achieve their new marks.

Next, when you ask something of your team, speak with conviction. If you are waffling in your tone or your direction, they will not take you or the task seriously. I also say "thank you" and "good job" whenever possible to let them know they are appreciated. It is important to keep morale high in your operation to make sure the train stays on track in the right direction.

Additionally, if you are asked a question that you don't know or don't want to answer offer a pivoted delay so you don't look clueless to your group. People don't expect you to always know the answer, but you have to seem like you are on top of it. Responses such as "Before I speak to that, let me check on something real quick and I will let you know" is much better then shrugging your shoulders with a quizzical look on your face.

If one of your people brings you an idea, don't chop it down before giving it a thorough chance to be heard. When they present their idea to you, it is a personal opening akin to placing themselves on the line. If you swat the idea without your people feeling heard, then the rejection will build to resentment and a dangerous low key enemy can be made. Case in point, Syndrome in the classic movie, "Incredibles" or Harold Jenkins from Netflix's "Umbrella Academy." They both wanted to help the heroes they felt a personal attachment to. When they were summarily rejected, the anger swelled into a bigger problem for the heroes than if they just took time to listen and be understanding.

Instead, pay attention to their presentation and if you like it, tell them that it is a good idea and how you can implement it with their contributions. If you're not sold on the idea, commend them on wanting to add value with their suggestion, but you won't be able to use their idea for reasons 1, 2, and/or 3. But, if we can work on that, perhaps we can do it in the near future. They will be happy they were heard and might even have an option down the road so it gives them a chance to contribute later. The point is to have people on your team that add value and think outside of the box to create fresh perspectives. Innovation is very important to staying ahead in The Game, be welcome to any source that provides it.

HIRING / FIRING

Always recruit the best talent available. Hiring someone is a task because it costs time and resources to get them up to speed on the operation, so you want to get it right. When you nail it, it is wonderful seeing that team member grow and become successful within your organization. Before you look at the candidates, however, know qualities that would work best for the position. Then find the one that best fits. Do not be intimidated if they may know more than you or have a greater skill because you want the best for the team.

On the flip side, if it is absolutely necessary to have to fire someone, thank them for their time and contributions while providing solid examples of why they are not going to be working there anymore. It can be an emotionally charged environment because few people enjoy inflicting the rejection and uncertainty of losing a job much less be on the receiving end. But if it must be done, do it sharp, clean and with empathy. Have understanding, speak facts, but do not raise your emotional level. It will not go well for either of you.

Since we are on the subject of addition by subtraction in your life, Jah offers this nugget, as a business owner, "you will learn who can and can't come with you. It's trial and error. Get people around you, feel them out, talk to them. People will sell you pipe dreams but when it comes to the action, they fall off. My patience runs thin and my energy is low dealing with things that don't make sense but if you remain resilient, like 'I gotta get this done, I gotta get this finished,' you will make it. But it is difficult."

LEADERSHIP STYLES

For me, I found it to be extremely important that your team sees you working in the trenches on occasion. This demonstrates that you are not too big to do the dirty work if necessary and that you will not ask anything of them that you will not do yourself. Plus, it shows how you want the task to be done. For example, I will take the trash out or move tables around if necessary. This is "Leadership By Example." Just make sure not to do it too often, otherwise why pay them to do it?

Jah agrees by stating, "I will never send another man to do something that I won't do. It keeps everyone motivated around you. We all work together, I'm nobody's boss."

There are 8 known leadership styles. Let's go over them and find one or a possible combination that fits your needs. Good leaders will have to employ several techniques on occasion depending on your personality and goals.

1. *Democratic Leadership*
   This leadership style has one leader that makes decisions based on input from each team member. Each team member has a voice, but the final decision usually rests with the leader. This works well because everyone gets a chance to be heard. This style can be seen usually at board meetings.

2. *Autocratic Leadership*
   This is more of a dictatorship style. The leader that takes on this role has a "my way or the highway" style. Dissent is not tolerated and no input from team members is taken into account.

3. *Laissez-Fair Leadership*
   Laissez-Fair is French for "let them do." With this style, leadership lets the team do what they want and yields all authority to the unit. There are few restrictions on how the work gets done and thereby, if it gets done. So, it is important that if you utilize this style there is a system in place to make sure the work actually gets done.

4. *Strategic Leadership*
   This leader acts as the bottleneck between upper management and staff. They accept the pressure from the top to get things done while empathizing with the workers downline on how to get it done. In effect, they straddle the fence and are the very definition of middle management. The idea of advancement is slim because they act as the buffer between the two worlds. Squeezed from both sides, they have nowhere to go so they will eventually end up in the same place.

5. *Transformational Leadership*

   With this style, a leader is constantly pushing the team past its usual set of tasks and goals. This leader sees the opportunity to always do better so they put the team on track to that end. If a team member can't keep up, they are usually left behind.

6. *Transactional Leadership*

   These leaders reward good work that is above and beyond with bonuses. The down side is that the team may hold out on their usual work unless they know that they will be rewarded extra. So, be sparing in your rewards.

7. *Coaching Style Leadership*

   This style recognizes that each team member brings something unique. It is up to this leader to get the best out of each member's skill set through constructive team building while heading towards a common goal.

8. *Bureaucratic Leadership*

   This style is strictly by the book. The thought of the organization is that it has worked for us this long, so it will continue to work for us. As a result, innovation is discouraged because it goes against the company policy. Do not disrupt the machine or you will be ground to dust by it.

The best leaders lift people up rather than tear them down.

POOR LEADERSHIP QUALITIES

Just as there are great leaders, there are some that will lead you off a cliff if you let them. Here are some qualities that make poor leaders.

1. *Lack of Flexibility*

   As Bruce Lee teaches, "you must be like the water. Water flows into the cup, it becomes the cup." If a leader has no flexibility then they cannot make timely moves that allow the best chances of success. Plus, a good leader will need different approaches with different team members. One size does not fit all in the leadership department.

2. *Self-Centered*

   If you make it all about you, the team will not respond well and they will not be properly inspired. Share credit where it's due and make it a team effort. There's no "I" in team, remember?

3. *Lack of Empathy*

   If you are unable to put yourself in the shoes of your team, then they will reject you. You must be able to connect with your crew by understanding their perspectives, what it is you are asking of them and their challenges (professionally and personally). If you can connect with your team on a deeper emotional level by making them feel valued, they will do everything in their power and beyond to accomplish anything you ask.

4. *Lack of Vision*

   The best leaders keep an eye on the future and bring innovation and growth to the unit. Status quo and being in a comfort zone are detrimental to your cause. If your team does not believe in your vision, then it is just a job and they will treat it as such. You must paint a big picture of success for your team that they will actively reach for day in and day out.

5. *Lack of Enthusiasm*

   Your team will take on the personality of its leader. If you do not come into work every day with a smile, energy and a hunger to get the most out of the day, then you cannot expect your team to do the same. A lack of enthusiasm translates into a pessimistic attitude that will poison your organization. They will feed off of your energy. Like The Rock says, you must "bring it" every day!

6. *Lack of Trust*

An organization with no trust is one that will not be able to grow. You must trust in your people that they will deliver the goods in their tasks and business decisions. Yes, trust will take time and it will be hard with a project as important to you as this, but it is necessary. If you watch them like a hawk or micromanage, your people will be uncomfortable and unable to perform the tasks you are asking of them. Build trust incrementally, but build it you must.

7. *No Integrity*

Integrity is a necessary building block for your people to be able to follow you. Being honest and of high moral principles is essential to building a company the right way. Plus, your team has to believe in you following your words with congruent actions. Yes, you could cut a corner or two but it will always catch up in the end. A company built on bad business will eventually fold with everyone looking out for themselves. Ask Jordan Belfort aka, "The Wolf of Wall Street."

8. *Poor Communication*

Leadership is about direction, guidance and support. All of which rely on effective communication in order to operate efficiently. Bad communication means that the ideas that you have in mind aren't being articulated correctly leading to confusion and missteps that you can't afford.

9. *Lack of Culpability*

Yes, even you mess up. It is important to use this as a teachable moment to your team to show that you make mistakes as well. But, also show

how you made up from the mistake, learned from it and moved forward. Just don't make too many mistakes or your people will lose faith in you.

WARNING

Be aware and always mindful of the team member that constantly does a power check. This is the one that will consistently question your authority. There is a difference between asking for further directions or proofing to see if the plan has any holes. This hater is the one that feels they could do it better than you but won't step up to the plate directly. Rather, they will throw jabs or low key shots in your direction to test your mettle.

It is important that you check this quickly or they will rally others to their side against you. People crave direction and tend to follow the loudest voice in the room. Even if as Frank Lucas notes in "American Gangster," "the loudest one in the room is the weakest one in the room." How valuable they are to the team dictates to what degree you should handle them. You can hit them with facts, boss check them in front of everyone, pull them to the side or fire them completely. But, handle them you must or risk an eventual insurrection.

* * *

NOTES TO SELF // TODAY I LEARNED ... // MY NEXT STEP IS ...

13

TAKING AN L

"Our greatest glory is not in never failing, but in rising up every time we fail."
RALPH WALDO EMERSON *(Poet)*

===

"You, me, or nobody is gonna hit as hard as life. But, it ain't about how hard you hit. It's about how hard you can get hit and keep moving forward. That's how winning is done!"
ROCKY BALBOA, *"Rocky Balboa"*

===

"Everybody has a plan until they get hit in the mouth."
MIKE TYSON *(Heavyweight Champion Boxer)*

===

"Sunny days wouldn't be special, if it wasn't for rain / Joy wouldn't feel so good, if it wasn't for pain
Death gotta be easy, 'cause life is hard / It'll leave you physically, mentally, and emotionally scarred"
50 CENT - *"Many Men (Wish Death)"*

===

"I have not failed. I've just found 10,000 ways that won't work."
THOMAS EDISON *(Inventor)*

===

"Victory has many fathers and defeat is an orphan"

JOHN F. KENNEDY (*35th President of The United States*)

The journey towards success in The Game is not an easy one or a straight line. Often, there will be times when you have to take a loss also known as an "L." Some may be more painful than others, but rest assured, there will come a time when you will experience it. The trick is, when you do, how do you handle and recover from it? If you are not careful, it will take you down and prevent you from getting back to a winning streak. Remember, you cannot help what happens to you, you can only help how you react to it. You can let it sink you or you can get up, learn from it and move forward, the choice is yours.

Personally, I have taken my fair share of L's. There was the time that I lost my Mother to cancer and I couldn't afford to bury her. I once put all of my eggs in one basket with a $380,000 contract on the table for a series of Australian and Southeast Asia tour dates that I knew was going to hit only to be sabotaged at the last minute when the funding fell through unexpectedly. Another time right after we paid our rent with deposits for upcoming events, the roof at The Venue caved in and we had an indoor waterfall during a storm rendering the building unusable. Or once after all the time invested, promo work and paying for artists consumed all of the cash, only a few people showed up to a concert. Yet, we still had to pay the law enforcement security and back half of the building rental fees because the money budgeted was spent unknowingly by a janky business partner of the cloth. I even dealt with heartbreak when I thought I was on the cusp of having it all. No way around it, life can really throw some tough shots.

Each event and others that weren't mentioned were devastating in their own way. The key is to understand that pain does not last always and you must learn to let it go. Understand that the strife added to your life can be a positive. There cannot be greatness without struggle. And you will never carry more burden than you can shoulder. You must not dwell on the how's and why's of what took place but instead focus on the fact that the L took place, accept it and learn from the lessons that it teaches. Then the L is not a mistake, it is an opportunity for growth.

Taking L's is not exclusive to me. Imagine putting together the Cash Money deal - at the time, the largest deal in the music industry that clocked in at over $30 million and you have to sue to get your fair share. That's what happened to Wendy Day. "I was really proud of that deal because it was just me and my lawyer negotiating it. We worked out an 80/20 (distribution) split, $30 million deal that advanced to $70 million 20 months in. I worked for free for three months and cash advanced my credit cards so I could live knowing the deal would get done soon. When they didn't pay me, my life spiraled. I got evicted losing out on baby pictures and pictures of my recently passed Dad."

She continues, "but the great thing about it is that there are things in life that test you. I never had a time where I said I didn't want to do this anymore. It never soured me from helping other artists. Yes, it hurt my feelings but it never impacted me mentally. It never stopped me. I feel as though I was tested and I passed. Time heals everything and I eventually got my check."

Or in the case of Uncle Head imagine learning that The Game, "was a cut throat experience when you are getting got from your label and the one handling your show money, so I had to learn the business." He goes on to say, "get your publishing, handle your business and you will be ok."

Don't get me wrong, you are allowed time to grieve and be upset. But, only take one day, maybe two for your pity party. Because the sun will come up tomorrow for another chance at greatness. If you are unwilling or unable to meet the challenge, all of the work you have put in to this point will have been wasted. If you are emotionally invested in the past or focused on what tragedy took place, you will not be in a position to take care of the present or set up your future. Understand that life is not fair, nor will it ever be. The sooner you accept that what happened has happened, the sooner you will be able to bounce back from it.

Zakiya Alta Lee advises, "you will always feel better when you focus on finding the solution and not the problem. In life you are going to go through things, ups and down. You just feel better when you are in a positive mood. With the Law of Attraction, you know that you will attract what you are. My spiritual life is huge for me. When you focus on a loftier view point, negative things don't matter so much."

Briefly, the Law of Attraction states that you will bring within your sphere of influence what you request of it. Meaning, if you put out positive vibes, you attract positive people and opportunities. Conversely, if you put out negative vibes, the contrary takes place. Read the fascinating book, "The Secret" by Rhonda Byrne for a more in depth analysis.

There are 5 stages of grief when you take an L. There is no particular time frame on which you will complete them, but you will need to go through them in order to keep moving forward.

1. **Denial** – "This can't be happening to me!"

2. **Anger** – "This is some bull…, it's all your fault!"

3. **Bargaining** – "If we give them this, maybe we can get them back to the table."

4. **Depression** – "All that work up in smoke, I need a drink and some me time."

5. **Acceptance** – "It is what it is, let's learn from it and move forward."

Understand that you are not the first, nor the last that will ever take an L in The Game. But, this particular L experience is unique to you and only you can carry it. It will take a strong mind, spirit and a great support system to get through it, but you can do it. In fact, you MUST do it in order to be successful. US Founding Father and inventor, Ben Franklin stated, "only by enduring pain may greatness be gained." Just because a venture fails, it does not make you as an individual a failure. Things happen, but how you recover is what matters the most. Plus, a valuable by product of when you come through the storm will be the respect you gain from your peers and enemies who are watching to see how you handle adversity. In addition, you will gain the armor of knowing that experience will not harm you again, strengthening your resolve.

Do not make any serious decisions while you are going through this emotional roller coaster. It will be very easy to make a bad decision and compound the L. Take your time, reassess after the crisis and then decide what the next best course of action will be.

If you have employees that are depending on an opportunity that has now turned into an L, you MUST NOT and CANNOT be seen sulking or having the body language as if this is the end of the world. They will lose faith in you and therefore in any future plans to bounce back going forward. Morale is extremely important in this delicate time. You must carry on as if everything will be ok (especially if you are in the middle of all hell breaking loose). They will look to you for leadership and guidance. If you fail them on these fronts, it will be extremely hard to get them back because they will see you as weak. If you need to, cry at home but never in front of your troops.

DJ Demp explains further, "a lot of times when they take a failure, it takes them out The Game. You gotta take those as lessons and learn to build on and keep going. You have to know how to maneuver. Stay true to what you are doing and stay focused. You're going to go through the trials and tribulations, if you are climbing a rock, you may slip but that doesn't mean you restart from the bottom. You have to keep going. That's how I got to Demp Week 23."

He continues, "I've dealt with so much nonsense, but I'm not going to let them see me sweat. You can't fold under pressure. Let things play out and you gotta keep your cool. You can't let the outside people know there's a problem, it ain't everybody's business."

Kobe taught us that failure can be a good thing. It shows you where you are weak and forces you to address it so you can get better. There is no way he wins 5 NBA Championships without facing his fair share of adversity. Early in his career, he once shot four airballs in a row to end a playoff game. His answer was to go back to the gym and work on it. The next year, those airballs turned into game winners. That Mamba Mentality should be yours as well. Don't dwell on the problem, get back in the gym and work on your solution.

"Great things come from hard work and perseverance. NO excuses."
— Kobe Bryant.

COPING MECHANISMS & THE BOUNCE BACK

For some, humor, reaching out to a friend, mentor or prayer is helpful to relieve the stress of a situation and take the sting out of an L. Others prefer to meditate, take notes or go to the gym. The important thing is that you cope positively. Negatively coping such as binging on TV, food, drinking or drugs is not only unproductive, but it could set you back even further, compounding the L.

TJ Chapman says, "it's all mental. Ok, so you tried something and it goes left or goes wrong. How do you look at it? Is the glass half empty or half full? Do you look at it as 'I lost, I'm a failure I can't do this.' Or do you say 'alright, that's why that happened, that's why it didn't work, that's why I got taken advantage of, but you know what, I get it. It wasn't a failure, it was a learning experience that I put into effect for the next time and I can finally win.' People look at it as failure, but you ain't never fail if you learned something from it, even if you lost. But if you ain't learned and you ain't take nothing, then you failed like sh!t."

He continues, "to win, we all gonna fail. We all take losses but it's all in how you use them. I ain't necessarily smarter or better than you, but I done bumped my head so many times it's cracked open. I can't keep bumping my head, I won't have no brains or blood left. You have to learn at some point and stop bumping your head. I took those lessons, learned from them and kept going and kept the faith. I lost my house, my car, the business. It's hard. It takes a special person to persevere to have the stamina, the patience or the belief or faith for this thing to happen. And not everyone is built like that."

Remember, even with what may seem like you taking the largest L of your life, you can bounce back. Oprah got fired and later built a multi-billion dollar media empire, Michael Vick lost millions on contracts and endorsements when he went to prison, but when he got out, there was a team waiting to sign and pay him. Now, he gives back by going on numerous speaking engagements to preach against animal cruelty and has thus rehabbed his image. T.I. got dropped from Arista. He reverted to his hustler mentality, bossed up and created the P$C "In The Streets" mixtape series and went store for store, selling them independently. He dropped "24s" with such street heat, Atlantic came calling with a few million to sign him because of his Grand Hustle. David Banner had his van that he used to traverse the country and record out of stolen. He lost everything. Yet, the next week he signed his $10 million deal with Universal, went on to sell millions and star in several movies.

Remember, it usually works out in the end. And if it hasn't worked out yet, no worries, it's not the end. Don't give up!

THE ART OF THE PIVOT

In boxing, to reduce the damage of an inevitable incoming blow, trainers teach to lean into the punch and pivot. This way the force of the impact won't be as bad. In The Game, you must learn to pivot or turn sh!t into sunshine in order to salvage a positive from a negative. I will give you an example.

When we were planning the TJ's DJ'S TASTEMAKERS CONFERENCE & OZONE AWARDS in Orlando, the host hotel decided to use that weekend unbeknown to us as the start of their long delayed remodeling project. Instead of a beautiful lobby for the captains of the music industry to congregate, sign-in and network, there was now a construction site with a hole in the ground sectioned off by wooden sheet rock that created a narrow walk way to the elevator. Despite our complaints, the fact remained that this disaster area was now the potential face of our event. Since the industry is a cruel and insidious mistress when it comes to gossip and spreading negatives, our passion project would be dead in the water if this were to be the first impression of our guests set to arrive within hours.

Keeping a cool head, I was reminded of my trips to New York and how promotional teams used construction sites to plaster posters of their projects. I used this idea to pivot the problem into a solution by opening our area to the labels allowing signage on the plywood. They clamored to have rights to be the first posters our Tastemakers saw when they walked in. By the time our guests arrived, there was so much signage up that it looked intentional.

"Keep On Pushin'" - **BUN B (UGK)**

Greatness has a cost. You must be willing to make the sacrifices and understand that there will be adversity. Taking L's is a part of The Game. You must pay the cost to be your own boss.

When Dr. Dre decided that he had enough of the antics at Death Row Records, the label he co-founded, the only way he would be released is if he gave up the ownership rights to the music that he created during that time. These included classics such as his own solo album "The Chronic," Snoop's "Doggystyle," and 2Pac's classic track, "California Love" along with everything in between. He decided to bet on himself and walked away with only his integrity and drive to create Aftermath Records. When many in the industry "Forgot About Dre" he released "The Chronic 2001." Soon after, he was the sound for the supergroup The Firm, signed Eminem and 50 Cent then created the signature Beats By Dre headphone line with Jimmy Iovine which positioned him as hip-hop's first billionaire when they were acquired by Apple. Meanwhile, the Death Row catalog was just purchased by Hasbro Toys for pennies on the dollar for the once invaluable and untouchable property. Dr. Dre paid the cost and reaped the rewards as his own boss on the bounce back. Now it's your turn.

E. Mackey offers this advice, "if the moves you make make sense to everybody then you are doing the same thing that everyone is doing and you won't be able to plot a path. So, you have to do what feels right to you, learn from your mistakes, keep pushing and don't give up. Always be a student, always keep learning. Most times the prize doesn't go to the best, it goes to the one that doesn't quit."

He continues, "you can endure but you have to be resilient. When you're taking hits and living out of your car like I've done. [When] everyone knows your name and your work, dapping you up in public but they don't know that you have to figure out where you're going to sleep or eat, you've got to understand that these times are temporary. It's not forever. You're not going to forever not always have your phone or lights off or not know when you're going to eat. You have to believe in your dream. You have to believe in your brand and value that and keep going. Resilience and endurance."

Remember, it is also possible for you to have done your very best, covering all the angles and yet still suffer an L. Unfortunately, that's just life. You must never dwell on it because there will be a brighter day. But, you have to look forward to it. So, no worries! Smile as you pick up the pieces, learn from the situation and move forward.

In fact, 2Pac said it best on "Smile":

"Smile in the future but through whatever you see, through all the rain and the pain, you gotta keep your sense of humor. You gotta be able to smile through all this bullsh!t. Remember that…Keep ya head up!"

* * *

NOTES TO SELF // TODAY I LEARNED … // MY NEXT STEP IS …

14

WHAT'S MY MOTIVATION?

"You need to git up, git out and git something / Don't let the days of your life pass by
You need to git up, git out and git something / Don't spend all your time trying to
get high
You need git up, git out and git something / How will you make it if you never even
try
You need to git up, git out and git something / 'Cause you and I got to do for you
and I"
OUTKAST - *"Git Up, Git Out"*

===

"Cee-Lo will just continue traveling his route without any doubt or fear
I know the Lord ain't brought me this far so he could drop me off here
Did I make myself clear?"
CEE-LO GREEN - *"Git Up, Git Out"*

===

"Keep ya head up, ooh, child, things are gonna get easier / Keep ya head up, ooh,
child, things'll get brighter"
2PAC - *"Keep Your Head Up"*

* * *

When you play The Game, it can be tough to keep moving forward. Sometimes we need a little push to keep the ball rolling. With all of the negatives that we may face in a day, it's good to have a place where you can go to re-energize with the positivity to keep moving forward. Let this chapter be a safe space for you that allows that.

This chapter is filled with mantras, poems, quotes, memes, phrases and other motivational topics that will shake the blues away and get you back on your mission. Keep in mind that just because you might be down, you are not out. Only you can keep you down. Things happen, but it's up to you in how you deal with it. Don't let a setback stop you from doing what you are meant to do. Get up, do what Taylor Swift says and "shake it off." Whatever you do, just keep moving forward.

In fact, Kristin Dungee explains, "[In The Game] you are required to be a self-motivator, so you are working by yourself. You have to have that drive internally, so your mindset needs to be aligned with your goals. Your mood affects your behavior. If you're not in a good mood, it will affect the money you're making. You have to constantly give yourself a pep talk."

In this moment, it is important to remember your 'why.' This is the reason why you are doing what you are doing. It has to be stronger than just a monetary motivation or glory. This is what pushes you through the difficulties, the hardships and the mundane. Write it down, keep a picture nearby so you will be reminded as necessary to keep it moving.

With that said, OG Magnum wisely notes, "I still don't know what I want to do when I grow up. Being an entrepreneur, you must have an attitude. If your focus is on wealth, then you have to renegotiate that goal with yourself. Because you must have passion, first. If you don't have the passion, you won't be able to get to that place. To do that level of work, just the chasing of money is not enough. Whatever it is, have a passion for it. Don't be ashamed of your passion. We need people with a passion for plumbing. Be proud of what it is you do. Be the best at it. Passion is what leads you to legacy."

The Japanese have an artform called, kintsugi. Within it, broken ceramics are carefully mended by artisans with a lacquer resin mixed with powdered gold, silver or platinum. The philosophy of this form is that breaks and repairs are a part of the object's history. The repairs are visible - yet somehow beautiful. Like kintsugi, just because we encounter hardships that may break us, as we heal and repair, the finished product will be beautiful.

As such always remember what Zakiya Alta Lee says, "you are enough!"

MAN IN THE MIRROR
[pointing towards the reflection in the mirror] "That's the toughest opponent you're ever going to have to face."
ROCKY BALBOA, *"Creed"*

===

"I'm gonna make a change / For once I'm my life
It's gonna feel real good / Gonna make a difference
Gonna make it right

I'm starting with the man in the mirror / I'm asking him to change his ways
And no message could have been any clearer / If you want to make the world a better place
Take a look at yourself and then make a change"

MICHAEL JACKSON, *"Man In The Mirror"*

You must look yourself in the mirror and understand, that is the only person in the world you are competing with. Your mission in life is to make sure that every day you look in the mirror, you are better today than you were yesterday. Do not worry about anyone else on social media, in your circle, or in a profile you read about. You run your race the best way you can. Everything else is a distraction designed to take you off the right track - your track. Focus on the one in the mirror. Make that person the best person possible each day and everything will be ok.

Fun fact, when you say inspirational things to yourself in the mirror, it becomes much more powerful, especially when you are standing in the yoga Power Pose. Feel free to try it using any of the following passages in this chapter.

T.I. - *"Motivation"*

"Haters better get on your job, tell 'em / Haters get on your job, ni₤₤a
It's motivation
Sucka ni₤₤a, get on your job / If you hatin' get on your job, ni₤₤a

Motivation / Ni₤₤az fakin' only gonna inspire
Motivation / All your hatin' is fuel to my fire
It's motivation / Ni₤₤az plottin' on the crown saw droppin'
It's motivation / Hey, but I ain't slowin' down and I ain't stoppin'

Motivation / Na'an ni₤₤a don't stop my show
Motivation / You ain't know I don't stop, I go
It's motivation / Sucka ni₤₤az, can't make me suffer
Just make me stronger and make me tougher / It's motivation"

* * *

"I'm good enough, I'm smart enough and doggone it, people like me!"
STUART SMILEY (*Saturday Night Live*

===

"Learning to love yourself is the greatest love of all"
WHITNEY HOUSTON - *"Greatest Love Of All"*

===

"If you want something you've never had, you must be willing to do something you've never done."
THOMAS JEFFERSON (*3rd President of the United States*

===

"Do or do not, there is no try."
YODA (*Jedi Master*

===

"Change will not come if we wait for some other person, or if we wait for some other time. We are the ones we've been waiting for. We are the change that we seek."
BARACK OBAMA (*44th President of the United States*)

===

"Whatever the mind of man can conceive and believe, it can achieve."
NAPOLEON HILL (Author, *"Think & Grow Rich"*)

===

"Nothing is possible until it is done."
NELSON MANDELA (*President of South Africa x Activist*)

===

"To be immortal, you must first live a life worth remembering."
BRUCE LEE (*Actor x Philosopher*)

===

"Don't do work seeking recognition, do work worthy of recognition."
ABRAHAM LINCOLN (*16th President of The United States*)

===

"The world is yours and everything in it / Get on your grind and get it!"

YOUNG JEEZY - *"Sky's The Limit"*

* * *

When I was on line to be a member of Alpha Phi Alpha, there were several inspirational messages we were "strongly encouraged" to memorize and embody. The one that stuck out to me the most was "Invictus" by William Earnest Henley. So much so that the concluding couplet is permanently etched on my arm as a tattoo because of how moving it is. Hopefully it means something to you as well.

Keep in mind that he wrote this poem as he was in the hospital being treated for the terribly painful disease of tuberculosis of the bone, also known as Pott's disease. The poem is about showing undivided courage in the face of death and keeping the dignity against all the hardships in life. Plus, Nelson Mandela used it to cope with his years in prison during the darkest days.

"Excuses" serves as a reminder to never have any reasons as to why you can't do something and "If" explains the great things that can happens when you finally can put everything together.

===

"INVICTUS" by **WILLIAM EARNEST HENLEY**

Out of the night that covers me,
Black as the pit from pole to pole,
I thank whatever gods may be
For my unconquerable soul.

In the fell clutch of circumstance
I have not winced nor cried aloud.
Under the bludgeonings of chance
My head is bloody, but unbowed.

Beyond this place of wrath and tears
Looms but the Horror of the shade,
And yet the menace of the years
Finds and shall find me unafraid.

It matters not how strait the gate,
How charged with punishments the scroll,
I am the master of my fate,
I am the captain of my soul.

===

"EXCUSES" by **UNKNOWN**

Excuses are tools of the incompetent, used by the weak to build monuments that lead to nowhere. Those who use them seldom amount to anything.

===

"IF" by **RUDYARD KIPLING**

If you can keep your head when all about you
Are losing theirs and blaming it on you,
If you can trust yourself when all men doubt you,
But make allowance for their doubting too;

If you can wait and not be tired by waiting,
Or being lied about, don't deal in lies,
Or being hated, don't give way to hating,
And yet don't look too good, nor talk too wise:

If you can dream—and not make dreams your master;
If you can think—and not make thoughts your aim;

If you can meet with Triumph and Disaster
And treat those two impostors just the same;

If you can bear to hear the truth you've spoken
Twisted by knaves to make a trap for fools,
Or watch the things you gave your life to, broken,
And stoop and build 'em up with worn-out tools:

If you can make one heap of all your winnings
And risk it on one turn of pitch-and-toss,
And lose, and start again at your beginnings And
never breathe a word about your loss;

If you can force your heart and nerve and sinew
To serve your turn long after they are gone, And
so hold on when there is nothing in you Except
the Will which says to them: 'Hold on!'

If you can talk with crowds and keep your virtue,
Or walk with Kings—nor lose the common touch,
If neither foes nor loving friends can hurt you, If
all men count with you, but none too much;

If you can fill the unforgiving minute
With sixty seconds' worth of distance run, Yours
is the Earth and everything that's in it, And—
which is more—you'll be a Man, my son!

* * *

MOTIVATIONAL SOUNDTRACK

These songs can help you get through a dark period and keep you moving
forward while providing a source of inspiration.

Sounds of Blackness - *"Optimistic"*
Bob Marley - *"Everything's Gonna Be Alright"*
Goapele - *"Closer"*
Soul II Soul - *"Keep On Moving"*
Trey Songz ft. Drake - *"Successful"*
Notorious B.I.G. - *"Juicy"*
Whitney Houston - *"Greatest Love of All"*
Kanye West - *"I Wonder"*
Kanye West - *"Spaceships"*
Jay-Z & Beyonce - *"Boss"*
Lupe Fiasco - *"Show Goes On"*
Outkast ft. Goodie Mob - *"Git Up, Git Out"*
Outkast ft. Cee-Lo - *"In Due Time"*
Pharell Williams ft. Jay-Z - *"Entrepreneur"*

CUTS TO KICK START YOUR DAY

Ludacris - *"Get Back"*
Lil Jon ft. Pastor Troy - *"Throw It Up"*
Kanye West ft. Jeezy - *"Wait Til I Get My Money Right"*
Rick Ross - *"Push"*
Rick Ross - *"Hustlin'"*
Jeezy - *"Standing Ovation"*
Soulja Boy - *"Turn My Swag On"*
Yola DG - *"Never Gon' Let Up"*
P!nk - *"So What"*
Kanye West ft T-Pain - *"Good Life"*

* * *

NOTES TO SELF // TODAY I LEARNED ... // MY NEXT STEP IS ...

15

LET'S MAKE A DEAL

"You don't get what you deserve, you get what you negotiate."
CHESTER KARRASS (Author)

===

"The music biz is like musical chairs / It's about where you standin' when the music stops spinnin'"
JAY-Z - *"Hollywood"*

===

"We making the crowd move, but we not making no G's, and that's a no-no"
ANDRE 3000 - *"Elevators (Me & You)"*

===

"The world is yellin' 'Hootie Hoo' but in my pockets nuthin but gum and lint"
ANDRE 3000 - *"Benz or Beamer"*

Deal making is the life blood of The Game. Although industry deals will be referenced in this chapter, no matter what lane you decide to work in, making deals is how you advance your goals and agenda. As such, this information will be applicable to you as well.

DJ Lil Boy expounds, "always keep it business. Being professional is a part of doing great business. Know your worth and make sure the other person knows your worth and at the end of the day put it to paper so you can get your finances in the end after you show your talent. It's less stress and makes you more secure. The worst feeling in the world is when you are on stage playing to the crowd showing your talent and in the back of your mind you don't know if you are going to get paid the right way."

You must be mindful of the opponent across from you. They are looking to take advantage of you to get the best deal for their side. No matter how friendly they might be, they are not your friend. In a proper negotiation, both parties must feel as though they left something on the table because unless there is a rare occasion, you are not going to get everything that you want. But, you want to get as many things on your terms as possible. How is that done?

Wendy Day, the architect of hundreds of several multi-million dollar deals explains, "it is all about leverage. The more leverage you have the better the deal. Remember, this is a business. If they see that you are progressing, their interest in you grows because it reduces their risk. This is not about talent, this is about making money. If you already have a fan base, it is easier to rise to the forefront and get the best deal possible." She also warns that, "a new artist can get shelved with a bad deal due to no leverage. [Another] new artist comes in with movement and the label shelves you because you aren't proven."

To work more in their favor for leverage, when Wendy Day was putting together the Cash Money deal, she "shopped them with a full business plan since they dropped 31 albums in a 6 year period." As a result, they got a great deal that was valued at over $30 million at the time of signing. "I learned through the Cash Money deal that Baby & Slim knew that ownership in the long term is what really matters." After all, "this is not a free industry. If you are going to do this seriously, you have to put money behind it and build campaigns. Not just do it and post it."

Day goes on to explain that, "you should go into a negotiation knowing what you will accept and what you won't accept. A negotiation is two people agreeing on what works best for each of them. I never allow my clients to give up their publishing. When I did the No Limit deal with Master P, we took advantage of Priority not thinking that hip-hop would go that far and he was able to keep his masters, which is a huge deal!"

Another example of leverage is provided by Julia Beverly when she books artists. "The artist has the power when it comes to shows. It is supply versus demand. There are only 8 weekend dates per month so they control how the business is handled." She continues regarding the contract, "good contracts are spelled out with not a lot of legal jargon. The key crucial items need to be spelled out clearly."

This brings us to the next point. In a proper negotiation, you must do your research. Know who it is you will be going against and use that to your advantage. What are their likes vs dislikes? What do they value? What kind of company do they work for? What type of deals are they used to signing? Do they honor the contracts that they sign? Any and all information is vital when going into any deal making opportunity. Everything is on the table and each move is carefully scrutinized. Plus, if the person likes or respects you, they may be more inclined to give you what you ask for.

If you don't have the proper leverage you may be inclined to take the first deal that is offered to you, also known as the "Sucka Deal." The Game is rife with artists that have signed the notorious bad deal contract. Megan Thee Stallion is one of the latest examples of that. When she was first coming onto the scene, she had no leverage and signed a bad deal with an independent label created by the pro baseball player, Carl Crawford. When she began to blow up with real money and opportunities coming her way, Crawford wanted his piece. She disagreed as to his part in her success. So, they went to court.

During the back and forth, Megan was unable to release music for almost a year, resulting in millions of dollars in lost income and opportunities just as she was taking off.

TJ Chapman adds, "no matter the deal, it's all about the leverage. Build your brand and creating value within yourself so you can build some sort of leverage to get things in your favor. If you got none, then you get none and you are at the mercy of whatever they want to do."

Be mindful of the deals that you sign. What you sign today may not be in your best interest in the near future if you do what you are supposed to do. Make sure that any agreement that you sign has room for you to grow. Remember, it's a lot easier to sign the deal you want than it is to get out of one that you don't.

Prince changed his name to a symbol not because it was fashionable. He did it because he objected to Warner Bros., his label at the time, from claiming ownership of his name and stifling his ability to release music on his terms. So, he rebelled by writing "SLAVE" on his cheek, changed his name to an unpronounceable symbol in protest and became the Artist Formerly Known As Prince until the contract expired. Once freed, he reclaimed his name, released music independently and made brilliant business moves such as bundling concert tickets with his CD so it counts as an album sale as well. Prince went on record with Rolling Stone to say, "record contracts are just like – I'm gonna say the word – slavery. I would tell any young artist…don't sign."

THE ART OF THE DEAL

The anatomy of a business deal is comprised of three basic components: the expected return, upside potential and downside risk. In other words, what do I expect to happen? What is the best case scenario? What is the worst case scenario? Ideally, the goal is to have a fair expected return with a huge upside and very little downside. Once a deal is struck, you must honor that deal. Make sure you get as much out of it as you are able to because you may not be able to renegotiate or break the contract.

TJ Chapman advises, "have knowledge about the deal you are making. If you don't have the right resources, get an attorney, CPA, business manager or another entrepreneur. Someone who knows better to help guide you. If you hire the right person, the money you spend you will get back in the long run because it will make the deal that much sweeter."

EXAMPLE - When molding No Limit Records, Master P employed this technique masterfully when he landed a consulting meeting with Michael Jackson's lawyer. He learned that Michael Jackson had the best deal in the music industry at around 30 points (meaning MJ received 30 cents on every dollar made from album sales) so he went to the source that arranged the deal. With the thousands Master P paid for that fortuitous meeting, he made back in millions with this new knowledge and understanding to help land the historic 80/20 distribution deal with Priority. Master P was now earning 80 cents per dollar and keeping his master recordings.

KNOW YOUR WORTH - In order for you to properly negotiate, you need to know and have an accurate understanding of what you bring to the table. Thoughts and feelings do not matter, it is what you can prove. The more tangible your worth (ie, facts, figures, endorsements) the better your chances are to get the deal you want.

EXAMPLE - In the early days of The Venue, we had structural damage that prohibited us from operating and the landlord didn't want to fix it. To add insult to injury, the landlord still demanded rent from us. Knowing our worth, I exercised a clause in our lease that legally allowed an option of refusal of rent payments due to negligence on their behalf. Knowing that we would not pay rent and we would squat so no one else could come in either, the landlord relented and fixed the issue with a discount on the next month for the inconvenience.

THE POWER OF SILENCE - In a negotiation, there is power in silence. Psychologically, humans have a need to fill silence. Use this to your advantage. Say your key point succinctly, then be quiet. Let your opponent fill the silence with details to hear their positions, pick their brain, counter offer or otherwise give you information that you can use against them.

LET THEM MAKE THE FIRST OFFER - The side that puts out the first offer is always at a disadvantage. The recipient then has the power to accept or decline. As such, get them to go first. If there is a stalemate ask, "so, what do you feel is a fair offer" and go from there.

NOT ZERO-SUM – To believe they got a good deal, most people feel they must win and the other side must lose. Unless you are talking about money only, the goal should be to create a good deal for both parties because it is the only sustainable way to do business on both sides and it produces the best long term returns for everyone involved.

This is the give and take part of the deal. Be fair and don't take any negotiation personally, but be firm. If you are to give up something, get something equitable in return. Both sides are trying to come to a proper understanding. Then follow Billy Beane's advice in the movie "Moneyball," "once you get the answer you want, hang up the phone." You don't want to lose the gains you made by over talking a point.

DISCOVER THE WHY – It is important to understand why each side wants to make this deal. Once you discover what this is, then it becomes easier to hone in on what they want and you can use it as leverage. A good way to open the dialog is, "in your perfect world, what does the ideal deal look like to you?"

AND IF I DON'T? – What is the worst case situation if this deal doesn't get done? The one with the true leverage is the one that can walk away. If you are not dependent on this deal taking place, then you have the power to stay as long as it makes sense. Do not be afraid to walk away versus signing a deal that does not make sense for you. The stakes are too high for you to jump at a deal that does not work for you.

EXAMPLE - When my business partner and I were mulling the offer to purchase an established trophy business, the current owner attempted to play hardball. However, in my research I knew he had multiple creditors, a landlord close to eviction and tax problems. We walked away from the deal and told him that we will be waiting for you to get shut down, buy all of your equipment and product to start our own company. Hence, United Trophies & Awards was born because we had the leverage and decided not to jump at a deal that didn't make sense for us.

GET CREATIVE – Sometimes you have to think outside of the box to get things done. When we negotiated the terms for The Venue, I put in stipulations that broke down the security deposit over three months because it would have been too much for us in one payment. Since we found a creative solution, the deal went forward when it could have been sunk due to financing.

KEEP IT SIMPLE – Tyler Tarr from Cutco taught me that "a confused mind will always say no." Keep your deals straightforward and simple. The more complicated it becomes, the less likely it will be a good deal for you. With that being said, make sure you understand everything in the deal. Go over it point by point if you have to, especially with your lawyer. Your life is on the line, act accordingly.

GET PERSONAL – The deal that you sign has a human representative that you will be working with after the deal is signed. Make sure you are on good terms with that person. In effect, you are in a business marriage. Keep the relationship strong.

BE A GRACIOUS HOST / OPPONENT - Even in a contentious negotiation, being a gracious host or opponent is important to keep you balanced and on good terms so that progress can be made.

KEEP YOUR EMOTIONS IN CHECK - Someone on an emotional roller coaster is not an attractive quality for a potential business partner. Plus, it clouds your judgement when you should be at your clearest. The only caveat to this is when strategically popping off will get a certain point across that will help in the long run. But, this is only to be used sparingly or it will lose its desired effect.

HAVE A UNITED FRONT - If you go in with a team, make sure everyone is on the same page and you have one point person going into the negotiation. If your opponent recognizes division, they will use that against you. If a point comes up that you must discuss as a team, politely ask for a sidebar. NEVER argue amongst yourselves in the negotiation. You will appear weak and will be taken advantage of. Cinematically, when Sonny Corleone voiced his disagreement with his father in a business meeting in the movie, "The Godfather," Vito Corleone got shot because their opponent found the weak point.

It helps tremendously to practice all of your talking points as well as potential counter points before the meeting. You only get one shot at it in real time, so make sure you are prepared.

* * *

NOTES TO SELF // TODAY I LEARNED ... // MY NEXT STEP IS ...

16

SHOW ME THE MONEY

"He who has the gold makes the rules."
SCROOGE McDUCK *"Duck Tales"*

===

"Cash rules everything around me, CREAM / Get the money dolla dolla bills y'all!"
WU-TANG - *"C.R.E.A.M"*

===

"It's not how much you make, but how much you spent"
BIG BOI - *"ATLiens"*

===

"I used to be like I can't wait 'til I get a million plus / Now I'm like, what the f*ck is a million bucks?"
T.I. - *"On Top Of The World"*

===

"Gonna say this and run / Under condition one
Promise me you gon' stack / Promise me you gon' ball
Promise me you'll invest / Three fourths of it all
(For what?)
So your kids' kids' kids can have some cheese / Can't get with it?
Get get get get get on your knees / Cause 'wealth' is the word (yep)
'Rich' is 'round the corner from the curb"
ANDRE 3000 - *"Hollywood Divorce"*

Before we begin, just to give a bit of background on my brother, Marcus Kennedy. Whenever our Mother wanted to make sure we had pizza money for the night, she would send him on a mission to go find change in the house to help pay for it. Even back then, he had a nose for getting money. Today, he has taken that interest and turned it into millionaire status. He is here to share with us some tips to help you get to your dream financial state.

KK: What have you been doing out in the world since finding all of that couch money?

MK: Yeah, there's always change under the couch [laughs]. I am an Industrial Engineer and I got my Engineering degree from Florida State University (Go Noles!). I interned every summer while in school and got a job with the company I interned for, Kraft Foods. After a few years, I left that company to work for Intel because I love computers and thought that it would be a great company to work for and I still do. My job right now is as the General Manager of the Gaming and E-Sports division. Along the way, I got my Master's Degree at Babson College, the number one school for entrepreneurial ventures in the world.

So, you have a background on all types of businesses?

Yeah, that was my corporate background. But on the side, because you know everyone's gotta have a side hustle, right? I have bought and sold businesses, started businesses and personal finance. Plus, I was a professional gamer for a little bit too. [*Side note: you want no smoke with Marcus on Super Smash Bros.*]

What are the pro's and con's of being an entrepreneur versus working for Corporate America?

161

The best pro about Corporate America versus being an entrepreneur is security. I've had a paycheck at least every two weeks since I was an intern. You don't get that guarantee as an entrepreneur. And that works for most people. But it's also like golden handcuffs. It's one of the things that just keeps you there. For an entrepreneur, the only check that you get is the one that you make until you get established well enough to begin drawing a paycheck yourself. But that's a big risk because the number one con of being an entrepreneur is that most of them fail. The most successful entrepreneurs out there have failed multiple times before they became successful. And if you're an entrepreneur you have got to be ok with that. You have to be ok with learning from your failures and trying to turn that into a success.

On the flip side, the biggest pro is that you don't have to worry about working for someone else. Everything that you do goes into your own pocket, you are your own boss but that also comes with the responsibility knowing that everything falls onto your shoulders. Most entrepreneurs end up working way more hours than those in Corporate America. I'll give you an example.

When I started up my personal finance company, I worked for Corporate America so after my normal 8-5 work schedule, on nights and weekends, I would get up and read. I studied for my financial licenses and certifications on my off times. On top of my 40-45 hours per week I had to go get clients, so I hustled working a hundred hours a week to build a business. And it was great because I was able to help people save and manage their money plus build their portfolios.

It was a great experience, but man it was a lot of work! I realized that I could not do that and have a family all at the same time. So, I sold that company off and just kept my Corporate America job.

What certifications do you have?

On the financial side, I got my Series 7 and Series 65, which lets you get paid to give financial advice. The Series 7 lets you manage people's money through the financial regulatory boards. I've got my Lean Six Sigma Black Belt, which means I know how to make things more efficient.

Sounds like you have done very well for yourself. I'm sure all of our readers want to know, how many comma's in the account?

Our net worth just crossed over a million this year. Yay!

When our readers are finally getting money in their pocket and after they take care of the IRS, what are some of the things they can do to keep their wealth?

You hit on one of the most important things with your taxes. Once you get to a certain place, taxes start eating up a lot of your revenue. And so the way you set up your business matters because you can keep more of your money if you set it up the right way. If you do it the wrong way, you can actually get taxed two or three times. Normal taxation should probably hit you for about a quarter of what you make.

[*Marcus brings up an excellent point about creating your business legally. First, make sure you obtain a business license by registering your business through your local state agency. Use Delaware if you want the most advantageous tax breaks - fun fact, it is not necessary to be a resident of the state in order to file. Next, go to irs.gov to obtain your EIN (Employer ID Number) which serves as your unique sequence that allows a business to operate in the US. Then be sure to stay on top of all receipts and paperwork.*

Additionally, there are 5 tax classifications to choose from when you start your business, each with their own advantages. Below is a brief description of each to help you decide which works best for you.]

SOLE PROPRIETORSHIP

A sole proprietor is someone who owns an unincorporated business by himself or herself. A sole proprietorship is the simplest and most common structure chosen to start a business, and there is no distinction between the business and owner. The owner is entitled to all profits and is personally responsible for all of the business's debts, losses and liabilities.

PARTNERSHIP

A partnership is a single business where two or more people share ownership. Each person contributes money, property, labor, or skill and expects to share in the profits and losses of the business. A partnership must file an annual information return to report the income, deductions, gains, losses, etc., from its operations, but it does not pay income tax. Instead, it "passes through" any profits or losses to its partners. Each partner includes his or her share of the partnership's income or loss on his or her tax return. There are three types of partnerships: general partnerships, limited partnerships, and joint ventures. Partners are not employees and should not be issued a Form W-2.

CORPORATIONS (C-CORPS)

A corporation is an independent legal entity owned by shareholders. This means that the corporation itself, not the shareholders that own it, is held legally liable for the actions and debts the business incurs. Corporations are more complex than other business structures because they tend to have more administrative fees and complex tax and legal requirements. Because of this, corporations are more common with established, larger companies with multiple employees. In forming a corporation, prospective shareholders exchange money, property, or both, for the corporation's capital stock. A corporation generally takes the same deductions as a sole proprietorship to figure its taxable income. A corporation can also take special deductions. For federal income tax purposes, a C-corporation is recognized as a separate taxpaying entity. A corporation conducts business, realizes net income or loss, pays taxes and distributes profits to shareholders.

The profit of a corporation is taxed to the corporation when earned, and then is taxed to the shareholders when distributed as dividends. This creates a double tax. The corporation does not get a tax deduction when it distributes dividends to shareholders. Shareholders cannot deduct any loss of the corporation.

S-CORPORATIONS

An S-Corporation ("S-Corp") is a special type of corporation created through an IRS tax election. An eligible domestic corporation can avoid double taxation (once to the corporation and again to the shareholders) by electing to be treated as an S-corporation.

S-Corporations are corporations that elect to pass corporate income, losses, deductions, and credits through to their shareholders for federal tax purposes. Shareholders of S-Corporations report the flow-through of income and losses on their personal tax returns and are assessed tax at their individual income tax rates. This allows S-Corporations to avoid double taxation on the corporate income. S-Corporations are responsible for tax on certain built-in gains and passive income at the entity level.

To qualify for S-Corporation status, the corporation must meet the following requirements:

- Be a domestic corporation
- Have only allowable shareholders including individuals, certain trusts, and estates and may not include partnerships, corporations or non-resident alien shareholders
- Have no more than 100 shareholders
- Have only one class of stock
- Not be an ineligible corporation (i.e. certain financial institutions, insurance companies, and domestic international sales corporations).

LIMITED LIABILITY COMPANY (LLC)

A Limited Liability Company (LLC) is a hybrid type of legal structure that provides the limited liability features of a corporation and the tax efficiencies and operational flexibility of a partnership. The "owners" of an LLC are referred to as "members." Depending on the state, the members can consist of a single individual (one owner), two or more individuals, corporations or other LLCs.

Unlike shareholders in a corporation, LLCs are not taxed as a separate business entity. Instead, all profits and losses are "passed through" the business to each member of the LLC. LLC members report profits and losses on their personal federal tax returns, just like the owners of a partnership would.

Since the federal government does not recognize LLC as a business entity for taxation purposes, all LLCs must file as a corporation, partnership, or sole proprietorship on their tax return. Certain LLCs are automatically classified and taxed as a corporation by federal tax law.

[Yay, now you are officially open for business! Make sure to always file your taxes, keep up with your paperwork and hire an accountant if it becomes too much. Marcus continues...]

But as Big Boi from Outkast said, "it's not how much you make, but how much you spent." You can make a million dollars a year, but if you spend a million and one, then you're always going to be in debt. So, the first thing you need to do is to figure out how much you spend and track it. It's really easy nowadays with apps like mint.com or Personal Capital or even just your banking apps. You might find out that you are spending way too much money eating at McDonald's or Guthrie's. In my case, we spent way too much money on Amazon deliveries. 10% of our income was going to that and we had to stop ourselves and say hang on, that's a lotta money we are spending.

Then [you can] figure out how much you want to spend. It takes discipline, but once you figure it out, you can begin to start saving money. If you don't get your spending under control, then you are going to have a big problem. Everything else will fall into place after that.

Entrepreneurs will sometimes go in debt with credit cards and loans thinking that this is only temporary and I will pay it back when my venture takes off. So, how do you manage debt?

First, don't go into debt. It's easy to borrow money when it's a bunch of zeros and commas on a computer screen until you get the credit card bill and it's overwhelming. So, the easiest way to manage debt is to not borrow anything. I would recommend as an entrepreneur to save up money first and use cash first and foremost. If you don't have the cash right now and you have to borrow, do it with the lowest cost possible, which is friends and family first. There's a reason that's where the richest people in the world will start. Like right now in Silicon Valley, where you have venture capitalists go around and collect money from other people to get started. They know it is cheaper and easier to do it at a 10% return then to run up a credit card at 30% a year. By the way, credit cards charge you by the day, so that 30% is divided by 365 days, so by the end of the year that 30% is actually 50% and they hit you over the head with credit card debt. So I would say that credit cards should be the very, very, very, very, very, very last thing on your list to get money from. Keep asking for funding until you find someone that believes in your vision.

The second thing I would say is if you need to save up, get a second job. There's a reason why a lot of people chasing their dreams bus tables or work fast food. There's no shame in doing what you need to do to support your dream. You have got to pay your bills too. You can stay hungry, but you don't want to starve and die, right? So, I would suggest having a minimum job that allows you the flexibility to chase your dream.

If someone has made mistakes with their credit or got into debt, what are some quick things they can do to minimize the damage or get out of it all together?

First, you have to figure out how bad is the debt so you want to pull your credit report and get your FICO Score. There's lots of free places to do it such as [annualcreditreport.com or call 1-877-322-8228]. Your FICO Score is the report that companies, who you might want to borrow money from like credit cards or banks, will use to see how trustworthy you are with money. That number is a three digit score that will tell them how much they should charge you when/if they lend the money to you. Two points could make a difference between you paying an extra thousand dollars a year. So, it's really important to know where you stand with your FICO Score. You are allowed one free one per year, but if a company pulls your report, you are allowed by law to request the report as well and get a copy that way.

Your score will be lower if you've got a lot of outstanding balances or if you haven't been paying your bills and you've made those mistakes we talked about earlier. And it will be higher if you have been paying your bills on time and haven't kept a lot of high balances. Anything on your report can stay on there for seven plus years.

If you have outstanding balances on your report, talk to the collection agency who will negotiate with you to pay off an old debt for pennies on the dollar. You will see your score start to skyrocket and then you can borrow money more cheaply. Keep in mind though with student loans that never leaves your report, so make sure you pay them off.

Once you start getting money, what can you do to make it work for you?

Cash flow is king. First thing, once you get your spending under control is now you can start to save. Get a separate account other than the ones for your bills so you can actually see it start to grow. Even if you keep it under your bed or a piggy bank. Then you can begin to invest it. Companies like Ameritrade,

Robin Hood, or one of these online brokers can put it somewhere and you can buy a piece of any company like Amazon, Tesla or Intel and watch your investment grow as you share in their long term growth.

Plus, there is a cool thing called compound interest. If you let your money sit in an account, it just keeps growing and growing. And the stock market averages growth between 7-9% per year. So the longer it stays in there, the more it keeps growing.

Real estate is good too, but it can be a real pain being a landlord sometimes.

And if you have money and you want to put it toward something? First figure out what you're saving for and keep saving until you can pay it off.

Any last minute Rules for the people?

Remember cash flow is king whether you are a really big corporation or you are a smaller entrepreneur. Always know where your money is going, figure out what you want to do with it and build towards your dream.

KEITH'S BONUS TIPS

As an entrepreneur, it is a relief to know that a check is on the way. And it is great to know how that check will be allocated once you receive it. However, under NO circumstance are you to spend money you do not yet have. You will be promised checks that you may have to end up spending extra time tracking down or worse, never receive at all. If you spend it before you tangibly have it in your possession, you will be making an extremely risky financial decision.

Once you receive a check and need suggestions on how to properly spend it, try using this winning formula that works for me. Feel free to adjust the percentages as needed, but the important thing is that you put money in each category with each check:

- 50% - Bills and every day spending (rent, utilities, gas, groceries, etc.)
- 20% - Pay Yourself - buy yourself something nice within budget, you earned it! My Uncle Clyde suggests you at least take yourself out to eat once every payday.
- 10% - Oh Sh!t - your rainy day fund for when the unexpected happens
- 10% - Savings - untouched money that sits and accumulates interest
- 10% - Reinvestment / Future Spendings - future big spending plans or investments

The Notorious B.I.G. adds on "10 Crack Commandments," "Rule Number Uno, never let no one know / How much dough you hold cause you know / The cheddar breed jealousy / 'specially if that man f*cked up, get yo' a$$ stuck up!"

Lastly, as Jay-Z stated on "Never Change" "chains are cool to cop, but more important is lawyer fees." It's understandable when you get your first piece of the pie, you wanna ball out a lil bit. But, make sure you have your business in order first. Lawyers and accountants will help keep you on task as you make moves in The Game. Find a good one and make sure you get value out of what you pay them.

===

If you would like to get personal financial advice from Marcus Kennedy, email info@rulestothegame.com.

* * *

NOTES TO SELF // TODAY I LEARNED ... // MY NEXT STEP IS ...

17

MIND, BODY & SPIRIT

"If you look good, you feel good and if you feel good, you play good."
DEION SANDERS (*NFL & FSU Hall of Famer*)

===

"Pain is weakness leaving the body!"
THE ARMY

===

"Your focus determines your reality."
QUI GON JIN - *"Star Wars, Episode I"*

In order to achieve the success that you are looking to attain, you must have a strong personal core. Your mind, body and spirit are the essential elements of you. They are the engine that keeps you on track. Conversely, if you don't take care of them, they could be the reason why you fall off. You cannot win at The Game if you do not keep your mind, body and spirit healthy.

Of course, depending on where you are in your journey, there are varying degrees on what is most effective. However, the earlier you develop healthy habits, the better your chances are to take full advantage when you apply them to your life. If you haven't been living the best way, do not despair, today is the day you start to take better care of yourself.

DISCIPLINE

Before we get into tips and philosophies, the first thing you must develop is your strength of discipline. To achieve your glory, you must utilize and practice these techniques every day for them to be useful to you. Arnold Schwarzenegger didn't develop strong strong muscles to be the youngest Mr. Olympia ever by only going to the gym when he felt like it. No, he had a discipline that had him eating right, working out, and putting in the time daily to get better and achieve his dream of becoming a champion.

With discipline, you are strengthening your self-control. And if you have control of self, you will have an advantage in whatever arena you choose to enter. Plus, statistically, those with greater self-discipline that can control their willpower lead happier lives because it will be on their terms.

This is not an easy process, especially in the beginning. It is a day by day practice, which is the hard part. But, it will get easier the longer you do it. However, you must decide to. There will always be two opposing forces that will help you do the right thing or tempt you to do the wrong thing, but it is up to you on which side you indulge. To this point, I will share with you an ancient Cherokee parable from my Native American heritage (thanks, Mom!) that best illustrates this.

An old Cherokee is teaching his grandson about life. "A fight is going on inside me," he said to the boy. "It is a terrible fight and it is between two wolves. One is evil – he is anger, envy, sorrow, regret, greed, arrogance, self-pity, guilt, resentment, inferiority, lies, false pride, superiority, and ego."

He continued, "The other is good – he is joy, peace, love, hope, serenity, humility, kindness, benevolence, empathy, generosity, truth, compassion, and faith. The same fight is going on inside you – and inside every other person, too."

The grandson thought about it for a minute and then asked his grandfather, "Which wolf will win?"

The old Cherokee simply replied, "The one you feed."

Which wolf will you feed today?

Here are a few techniques that will help you feed the right wolf and strengthen your resolve.

1. ***Know Your Weaknesses*** – Once you acknowledge them, you can work to diminish them so they don't cripple you or your enemies using them against you.

2. ***Remove Temptations*** – If you remove the bad distractions from your path then you will be less likely to be negatively influenced by them.

3. ***Set Clear Goals & Have An Execution Plan*** – Once you know what your target is and the way to achieve it, then all you have to do is execute the plan. If you don't have a plan then it is much easier to fall back into your old ways.

4. ***Build Your Self-Discipline*** – It is not a sexy topic, but you must take pride in making the right decisions. Each right decision, builds on the last one and before you know it, your willpower will be unshakable.

5. ***Make It Easy To Create New Habits*** – Keep your actions into small doable steps. One step at a time is how you climb a mountain.

6. ***Eat Often & Healthy*** – You can't make the right decisions with a growling stomach or one filled with poor nutritional value. How far will

your car go with cheap gas or none at all? Give yourself a fair chance by having the right fuel.

7. ***Don't Limit Yourself*** – Do not put artificial limits on yourself with negative thinking, such as "I will never be able to do that." Whether you think you can do it or think you can't do it, you will be right. Don't block yourself before you get a chance to see how great you can become.

8. ***Reward Yourself*** – Make sure you take the time to see how far you have come and grant yourself permission to enjoy the work you have put in. But after a brief respite, get back to business.

9. ***Forgive Yourself & Move Forward*** – If you relapse, know that it is ok. Nothing that is worthwhile comes easy. Reset and begin again. You can do it!

MY PERSONAL EXAMPLE

My entire life, according to the doctors, I have had a weight problem. I have always been on the heavier side of what the health experts say I should be. At the time, I never saw it as a problem because I was somewhat athletic, I had charisma and I generally felt good, especially around the 215-220 lb mark. So, when I could eat a whole pizza by myself or down a heavy breakfast after the club or if I used food like ice cream or donuts as a way to cope when things got bad, I didn't see a problem. That is until one day I looked up and I at my heaviest weight, a rotund 245 lbs! My brother pulled me aside and showed concern about my health, so I decided to do something about it. It's funny, you don't realize how far you have gotten out of control until a loved one points it out or you don't like the person you see in a picture or mirror. The reflection never lies.

I went to the gym, ate right with the Subway diet and worked hard to get down to about 205. Then over time, I got complacent, poor habits kicked back in and my weight jumped up to 225 around last Thanksgiving. This time, my Alpha line brother Joe Paul, fresh from his health awakening pointed out all of the bad food I was eating at breakfast with disgust. Now at 40+, my health was at risk and if I didn't make changes now, I could have long lasting detrimental effects. This time, I was determined to lose the weight and keep it off.

I stopped eating late, I took up swimming, running (I've finished three 5k races!) and look forward to my gym time. I practice yoga, meditation and found an app, LoseIt! that helps me stay accountable towards my weight loss goals. As of this writing, I am now at 195 (-50 lbs and counting from my heaviest weight) which, by the way, is less than my high school weight. I weigh less now than when I crossed Alpha in college; and I had step practice every night back then to keep me in the best shape!

It was not easy, but once I made that determination and made an active decision to take care of myself, I built the discipline one day at a time to accomplish my goals. You can too!

HOW TO TAKE CARE OF YOUR MIND, BODY & SPIRIT

Your mind is where it all begins. If you have a healthy positive mindset, the world is a great place and you can do anything. But, if your mindset is negative all you will be able to see is the darkness and it will be tough to even get out of bed. The Law of Attraction in powerful. Plus, this Game will run you crazy if you let it. But, here are a few options that can help you stay in a positive light.

1. **Be Mindful Of Social Media** - Yes, it is a great networking tool and a way to communicate with friends and family. But, it has been discovered that paying too much attention to social media actually can put you in a depression. People don't post their negatives online, only their

positives. And even then, it is often a false positive. So, naturally when you compare yourself to the online best version of people, folks have a tendency to get down on themselves and their life. Don't compare your race to anyone else's. And especially, the virtual version of their life. It's unlikely to be the truth and that's being unfair to yourself.

2. ***Accept Yourself For Who You Are*** - We are who we are. Yes, we can make changes to be better versions of ourselves. But, when we get down on ourselves for other's ideas of what is good or beautiful, we will never be happy. Dr. Seuss said it best, "those that mind don't matter and those that matter don't mind." Live your truth and love yourself for who you are.

3. ***Eat Right*** - Once again, your body needs the proper fuel to keep moving in the right direction. It is easy as we get busy to grab the quickest and cheapest options. But, understand that you will pay for it in the long run. Fast food can lead to depression and long term health issues if you consume too much of it. Plan your meals and make the right choices so your body can keep going in the right direction. DJ Princess Cut suggests a "vegetarian plant based lifestyle because you live longer. Health is wealth. [You will] feel better and look better."

4. ***Keep A Positive Circle*** - The ones that are closest to you will serve as your support group. You will lean on them in the tough times and celebrate with them in the good times. Make sure they are positive people and have your best interests in mind. If they don't, drop them. It is not worth it to have negative people in your circle.

5. ***Be Grateful*** - Each morning, night or during quiet moments, you must count your blessings, at least 5-10. Your gratitude, even for the smallest things will put you in the mindset of appreciation that will do wonders for a positive outlook on what you have and not on what you don't have. Zakiya Alta Lee expounds by saying, "don't focus on what you don't

have, focus on what you do have. Focus on the opportunities in front of you. Sometimes we get caught up chasing what we don't have that we don't see what we have in front of us."

6. *Find A Hobby* - Find activities outside of your normal work or home life that will open your mind to creativity and/or keeps you active. If you focus on The Game alone, you will burn out quickly. It is important to have your mind refresh on activities that reduces the stress in your life.

7. *Giving Back* - Finding a humbleness in giving back or paying it forward is important because it makes things not about you. It gives a chance to help others which in turn makes you feel good by being empathetic to someone else. Plus, if you live in abundance, it is only right to help the next one behind you. Otherwise, your blessings will disappear. Zakiya Alta Lee agrees by stating, "I think it is important to take the tools that you have learned and pass it on to others so they can take it forward from there."

8. *Focus On What You Can Control* - It makes no sense to frustrate yourself by getting upset over things outside of your control. Alcoholics Anonymous has it right by their signature prayer, "God, grant me the serenity to accept the things I cannot change, the courage to change the things I can, and the wisdom to know the difference." It will save you tons of stress when you let go and only work on the things that you know you are able to change. After all, Zakiya Alta Lee notes, "we only have so much energy, do things that will work in your favor - choose your battles wisely."

9. *Pray or Talk To Someone* - Prayer changes things. It is true. But, if prayer isn't your thing, make sure you talk to a professional or at least a good friend. It helps to unload all of the feelings and pressure that you may have to someone that is trained or just wants to help ease your

mental burden. Personally, talking with a therapist has done wonders for me (s/o LaToya Boyd at Learned Behaviors!).

10. *Exercise, Yoga & Meditation* - These three elements will boost your endorphin levels, calm your spirit, relieve stress and focus your mind which lead to happiness. But, you must set up a regular routine. One way is to get an edge each morning. "The Edge" is credited to my Uncle Clyde, fmr. Marine, where you do 20 push ups and 40 crunches to start your day. It will get you kick started and build your body at the same time. With exercise, yoga and meditation, even if you start small and add over time, you will gain an edge on your competition and your day. If you need an online yogi, I highly recommend Yoga With Adriene on Youtube and @kakeini on Instagram.

BONUS Kristin Dungee aka Kakeini suggests that "it is important for the entrepreneur to give yourself permission to rest and not feel guilty about it. Choose at least one day for your rest day. For me, it was necessary for my body to heal and recover."

WARNING

Be mindful about catastrophizing. It is the practice of building up in your mind all of the things that can go wrong. We tell ourselves these things with the thought that they are just preparing us for the worst. In actuality, what it does is raise our anxiety. Sometimes to the point where we become frozen or crumble in despair. Especially, when these thoughts turn into a self-fulfilling prophecy.

To work against this, first recognize that it is happening. Then tell yourself, yes, those things could happen and it would suck or what if it all works out, which is much more positive. Then focus on that outcome. If necessary, go for a walk or do a quick workout to sweat the negative out of your system. Do not fall victim to the future that hasn't happened. With the Law of Attraction, the universe follows your energy, positive or negative and makes it real. Which will you choose?

YOUR SPIRIT

The first law of thermodynamics, also known as Law of Conservation of Energy, states that energy can neither be created nor destroyed; energy can only be transferred or changed from one form to another. When it comes to spirit or chi, it operates the same way.

Energy is either positive or negative. We all have both forms and transfer that energy to others as well as it can be transferred to us. Think about it, remember the last time you got a hug and you felt good because of the positive energy that was transferred? Or conversely, you got into an argument and the negative vibe stayed with you long after the interaction?

DJ Princess Cut confesses, "I like positive energy. I'm allergic to negative energy. I like to be around fun and good energy. It's just in me to give those vibes back. Even if a negative thought comes, I find a way to think positive. It's hard sometimes but at the end of the day, it's less stress and I want to keep my hair, so overall I am a positive person."

Everyone has a right to explore their own belief system. But for me, I know that we are all connected. In my travels, I have come to understand that there is a higher power out there guiding us. Some may call it God, The Universe, Jehovah, Jesus, Allah or Dave, but whatever you decide to name it, there is an interconnection between all of us. In fact, Bigga Rankin credits "most of my blessings in this job, come from believing in God."

As such, be kind to one another and blessings will be bestowed upon you. Be unkind and although you may get away with it briefly, karma has a way of equalizing all misdeeds. Now, since we all have a guiding spirit, it is important that you listen to your spirit. It is the one that helps you with your "gut feeling." Trust it. Especially when it is raising alarms or pushing you in a general direction or pushing you to the unknown. Sometimes you have to go to the unknown in order to grow into who you are meant to become. Your spirit knows what makes you happy. If you ignore it, you can be stuck in a position that constantly drains your spirit and puts you in a bad place until you finally learn to listen, then act on it. Case in point, have you ever been at a job you hate or been around someone that just didn't seem right? That is your spirit telling you to keep it moving.

Your spirit is the one that talks to you in the quiet moments and tells you what you need to hear. Not necessarily what you want to hear. But, you must listen. And you must act. Otherwise, you will be forced to repeat the same behaviors or be stuck in the same mindless circles until you set your spirit free. Do not be afraid to take that first step. Your spirit is telling you about your path to your glory, learn to listen with an openness.

If you can't hear it, clear away your clutter. The Chinese believe in feng shui which is the removal of obstacles in an environment so the energy or chi can flow unencumbered. Bruce Lee taught, "you must be like the water. Water flows in a cup, it becomes the cup. Be like the water." Learn how to flow and embrace your spirit. Remove the clutter in your house, office and/or life and watch as your spirit becomes stronger.

You must also fan the flames of your spirit with peacefulness. Find a favorite quiet place and learn to listen. Your spirit is there, even if it may be bruised from hard times. It is there waiting to keep you on the right path. Learn to listen and do what it says.

If you are having trouble finding your inner voice, Kakeini suggests, "mindfulness is a skill that you must practice. Meditation allows you to focus on breath. Don't block out thoughts and stay grounded." She continues, the "benefit is when I get overwhelmed, it brings me back to a calm harmonious place. It is important to have a center of balance."

* * *

NOTES TO SELF // TODAY I LEARNED ... // MY NEXT STEP IS ...

18

RANDOM RULES

"What you're about to witness is my thoughts / Just my thoughts man, right or wrong
Just what I was feeling at the time, uhh / You ever felt like this, vibe with me"
JAY-Z - *"The Ruler's Back"*

These are a few ideas and thoughts that made great points but did not fit into the flow of the book. But, I felt they are still important enough to share. Hopefully they will serve as a source of inspiration to you as well.

- Learn to pick your battles. "The Art of War" by Sun Tzu teaches to only go into a battle once you are sure it is won. We only have so much energy, choose the right battles that are worth fighting. But, if you are to go into one, make sure it is won before it has even started. This is done by proper research of the topic and your opponent; as well as choosing the time and location of the battle. Your preparation will help tilt the odds forever in your favor.

- *"May the odds be forever in your favor."* - **THE HUNGER GAMES**

- Never play the "What If" game also known as "The Road Not Taken." It is unfair to yourself and it will drive you mad expounding on hypothetical paths. There is no way to know or correctly predict what would have happened had you went a different direction than the one you chose. Andre 3000 told us on "Int'l Players Anthem" that "spaceships don't come equipped with rearview mirrors." The only thing you can do is focus on the path you did choose and put in every effort to make it the best one for you. Otherwise you will be so focused on the past, you will crash in the present.

- Be the turtle. Keep moving forward. Change no matter how incremental is still progress.

- Luck is when opportunity and preparation meet mixed with perfect timing. You can do all you can, but until it is your time, the only thing you can do is be prepared for it. If you stay ready for your opportunity, you will never have to get ready. Akon took one and half years on the promo circuit before "Locked Up" took off. But when it did, he was ready with hits for days and now he is opening his own city in Africa. Always be ready because you can never control your time, only your preparation.

- *"Opportunity is missed by most people because it is dressed in overalls and looks like work."* - **THOMAS EDISON** (Inventor)

- Enjoy the journey, embrace the struggle and take time to appreciate the special moments. When you finally make it, you will look back at these times and appreciate it for building you into the person you have always wanted to be.

- *"When the strees is watching, blocks keep clocking / Waiting for you to break, make your first mistake / Can't ignore it. That's the fastest way to get extorted."* - **JAY-Z** "Streets Is Watching" .. Always be aware of your surroundings at all times as you make your next best move. One mistake could be your last.

- Do your research. Before you make any decision or jump into any action, make sure you learn all you can about it. An informed decision helps make the right decision.

- Success is a numbers game. The more opportunities you create through seed planting, the greater the chance you will hit. Tyler Tarr at Cutco taught me to treat your phone like your personal ATM machine. The more you dial, the more leads you generate, the more money you can make.

- Competition breeds excellence. You must find an enemy or competitor to measure yourself against. It is the best way for you to get stronger in your craft. Besides, if you ain't got haters, you ain't doing it right.

- Consistency is key. Once is luck, twice is coincidence, three times is a trend. Make sure you do the necessary over and over again. Then the fruits of your labors will begin to blossom exponentially.

- Word of mouth is *THE* best form of advertisement. It comes from a trusted source to the receiver and is not sullied with payments that dilute the message.

- This is a Game of smoke and mirrors. It is designed to make stars famous, not rich based off of the illusion of "realness." Act accordingly.

- Chubb Rock taught us on "Treat 'Em Right," always take time for your fans. Just as they can build you, they can tear you down even faster. I admired how David Banner, T.I. and B.o.B would always stay after the show and interact with their fans. Even Jay-Z took a picture with a friend of mine after a show. That's how you build a foundation that will last through your whole career.

- *"You are what your record says."* – **BILL PARCELLS** (Legendary NFL Coach). Good or bad, you are the result of your decisions. Excuses won't help, so own them and always aim to get better.

- You are the result of the average of the 5 people you spend the most time with. So, don't flock with turkeys if you want to soar with the eagles.

- Always under promise and over deliver. Leave clients amazed at how good of a job you do and you will never run out of clients.

- If an idea is an ember, let your passion be the fuel to stoke this spark into a raging fire of productivity. An idea is only as good as the execution of it. History is full of examples of people with great ideas that were never heard from. But, the ones that are remembered are the ones that have the fortitude to see them through. Just because you have an idea, it doesn't mean it is exclusive to you. Someone else could be thinking the same thing. Now the race is on to prove who can do it better. Do you want to be first, last or best? The great inventor Nikola Tesla got scooped by Thomas Edison many times because Edison knew how to handle paperwork and work the publicity angle. What do you want your story to be?

- Understand that you have no clue as to where an idea can take you. Follow through with it all the way. Even an idea that transforms into something else can be advantageous. Rubber, penicillin and the microwave were all discovered chasing a different idea. Be mindful not to share them too early and allow a non-believer to snuff it out before it has a chance to be fully formed.

- *"There is no success without sacrifice. If you succeed without sacrifice, it is because someone suffered before you. If you sacrifice without success, it is because someone will succeed after."* - **ADONIRAM JUDSON** (Missionary)

185

.. In order to win, you must give up something valuable at the alter of success. Whether it be time with loved ones, money, resources, physically, emotionally or something else, you cannot win without first giving something in return. The greater the sacrifice, the greater the victory.

- *"Everything you get, you've got to work hard for it!"* **NOTORIOUS B.I.G. ft METHOD MAN,** "The What"

- *"It is easier to ask forgiveness than to seek permission."* - **REAR ADMIRAL GRACE MURRAY HOPPER** (US Navy)

- *"To be the best, you've got to beat the best! (Whooooo!!)"* – **RICK FLAIR** (16x World Champion Pro Wrestler)

- *"Baby boy, you only as funky as your last cut / You focus on the past, Your ass'll be a has what"* – **ANDRE 3000** "Rosa Parks" … What you have accomplished is cool, but in The Game, it's always about what's next.

- *"If you are good at something, never do it for free."* - **THE JOKER,** "The Dark Knight"

- *"The only place success comes before work is in the dictionary."* – **VINCE LOMBARDI** (HOF Pro Football Coach)

- *"Learning begins with humbleness"* – **BUJU BANTON,** "Til I'm Laid To Rest"

- *"You miss 100% of the shots you don't take."* – **WAYNE GRETZKY** (HOF Pro Hockey Legend)

- *"A wise man told me never argue with a fool, people from a distance can't tell who is who."* – **JAY-Z,** "Takeover"

- *"Sometimes better to be thought dumb and remain silent than to open your mouth and remove all doubt."* – **DMX**, "It's On"

- We all have to start somewhere. I was an intern with TJ's DJs, Diddy was an intern for Andre Harrell at Uptown, Tupac was a backup dancer for Digital Underground. It's not where you start, but where you finish. Appreciate that you have your foot in the door and use that as a step up to get where you want to go.

- Never make an important decision angry, hungry, horny or under the influence. Your judgement is clouded but the consequences of a poor reaction are permanent. Clear your mind and the proper course of action will reveal itself.

- If someone takes the time to teach you, be respectful, quiet and listen to what they say. What you do with the information is up to you. You never know where one nugget of inspiration or knowledge can spark an opportunity or idea that will launch something amazing for you.

- *"If I have seen farther than others, it is because I was standing on the shoulder of giants."* - **ISAAC NEWTON** (Philosopher x Physicist). Find a mentor. The right one will shave many hard knocks off of your journey.

- *"Someone is sitting in the shade today because someone planted a tree a long time ago."* - **WARREN BUFFETT** (Financial Guru). Don't pull the ladder up with your advancements. It is your duty and obligation to reach back and help the next generation.

- When offering a challenge to your team, give them the what and when but allow space for the how. They will surprise your with their innovation and willingness to see the project through.

- *"Biggest thing to achieving longevity in this business is having the ability to constantly recreate yourself and evolve with the times. Otherwise you will go extinct like the dinosaurs."* – **TJ CHAPMAN**

- *"You can't win it if you ain't in it!"* – **STEPHEN KENNEDY** (The Best Father)

- *"The world is mine, but it's up to me to go get it!"* – **KEITH KENNEDY** (Author)

THROWBACK PICS

Bigga Rankin & Keith

Keith & Killer Mike

George Clinton & Keith

Keith, Rico Wade & TJ

Snoop Dogg & Keith

Keith, Tony Neal & Derek Jurand

Keith, Lil Jon, TJ, Tony Mercedes & Friend

TJ, David Banner & Keith

Mom & Son

About the Author

Keith Kennedy has dedicated his life to following his passions of writing, music, business and helping others help themselves. During his 20+ years as an industry vet including 14 years as the Vice President of TJ's DJs - the fabled music marketing company, he was blessed to be a part of music history by helping artists such as B.o.B, T-Pain, Rick Ross, David Banner, Plies and more achieve success through the legendary Tastemakers Only DJ/Music Conferences.

Following that, he has created talent showcases, hosted his own sports/entertainment talk show, wrote about numerous artists & executives, booked shows, opened up a trophy shop & event hall. Plus, he finds time to mentor the next generation while travelling for book signings and speaking engagements at stores, schools and universities.

On his down time, he loves to live his best life by exploring the world through travel, cooking, creating and watching the FSU Seminoles & Jacksonville Jaguars achieve victory. Additionally, he loves playing chess, Mario Kart 8, Fall Guys, Dungeon Defenders II, Rocket League and other video games with his brother and nieces. PS4 Gamer Tag @KeithK926 if you want to come get some too!

You can connect with me on:

- http://www.rulestothegame.com
- http://www.twitter.com/rulestothegame1
- http://www.facebook.com/rulestothegame.fb
- http://www.instagram.com/rulestothegame

Subscribe to my newsletter:

- http://eepurl.com/hd3osT

Also by Keith Kennedy

If you enjoyed "Rules To The Game" prepare yourself for the upcoming slate of projects from Keith Kennedy through Manifest Destiny Publications. Follow on IG for pending updates - @KeithK926

More Rules To The Game
The follow up to the wildly successful business book, "Rules To The Game."

Rules To The Game Mixtape
The audio version of Rules To The Game coming to you soon!

Reflections of The Heart
A collection of poems from the heart of Judith Fain.

College Days Swiftly Pass
A semi-autobiographical coming of age love story set on campus during the Southern hip-hop scene explosion in the '90s and '00s.

Top Seleckta
A choose-your-own adventure saga where you rise through the ranks and become the world's best DJ.

Seasons of Love

Will a summer love bloom like spring or will it fall to the winter of our discontent?

www.ingramcontent.com/pod-product-compliance
Lightning Source LLC
Chambersburg PA
CBHW072000090426
42740CB00011B/2015